# Meditations for the Lone Traveler

# Meditations
# for the Lone Traveler

The Life of Faith in a Changing World

Mark W. Hamilton

CASCADE *Books* · Eugene, Oregon

MEDITATIONS FOR THE LONE TRAVELER
The Life of Faith in a Changing World

Cascade Books
An Imprint of Wipf and Stock Publishers
199 W. 8th Ave., Suite 3
Eugene, OR 97401

www.wipfandstock.com

PAPERBACK ISBN: 978-1-5326-0211-5
HARDCOVER ISBN: 978-1-5326-0213-9
EBOOK ISBN: 978-1-5326-0212-2

*Cataloguing-in-Publication data:*

Names: Hamilton, Mark W., author.
Title: Meditations for the lone traveler : the life of faith in a changing world / Mark W. Hamilton.
Description: Eugene, OR: Cascade Books, 2017.
Identifiers: ISBN 978-1-5326-0211-5 (paperback) | ISBN 978-1-5326-0213-9 (hardcover) | ISBN 978-1-5326-0212-2 (ebook).
Subjects: LCSH: Christian life | Spiritual life—Christianity.
Classification: BV4501.3 H36 2017 (print) | BV4501.3 (ebook).

Manufactured in the U.S.A.                                        MAY 18, 2017

For Samjung, Nathan, and Hannah,
who travel along with me, always

# Contents

# CONTENTS

# Introduction

The chapters in this small book are lightly retouched talks given to university students in the United States, Croatia, and South Korea, including those of Abilene Christian University, Austin Graduate School of Theology, the Biblijski Institut (Zagreb), Korea Christian University (Seoul), and others. The prayers that accompany them often served other settings, or were written in the first instance for use here. The biblical texts are my own translation, in which I have sought to capture at least part of the literary power of the original. My hope is that these modest reflections on Scripture will serve the devotional lives of readers as they also seek the God whose word both remains forever (Isaiah 40:8) and brings life to desiccated ground and parched souls (Isaiah 40:10–11).

The reader may wish simply to read one at a time and to return to the next later when the mood or need strikes. My hope is that everyone who encounters these small meditations will use them as catalysts for new insights of their own. "Go and do likewise" never seemed more appropriate than here.

To frame this work, I point to the great American poet Robert Penn Warren, who wrote about the craft of poetry:

> I would say poetry is a way of life, ultimately—not a kind of performance, not something you do on Saturday or Easter morning or Christmas morning or something like that. It's a way of being open to the world, a way of being open to experience. I would say, open to *your* experience, insofar as you can see it or at least feel it as a unit with all its contradictions and confusions. Poetry, for me, is

not something you do after you get it fixed in your mind. Poetry is a way of thinking or a way of feeling; a way of exploring.[1]

Reading Scripture, much of which takes poetic form, is also a way of life. The ancient text offers many surprises, some challenging or downright aggravating, but all of them offering a path worth exploring with all of one's mind and heart, for that path leads to God. This small book may serve some as a companion on that path, perhaps as a pointer to some of the beauties along the way.

Like many others, I do not walk this road alone, but rather in the company of others. My family, friends, colleagues, students, and occasionally enemies have shown me the signposts and landmarks along the path, picked me up when I tripped, encouraged me when my spirit flagged, and helped me keep on walking. They still do. My students and friends at Abilene Christian University, and especially my assistant Josiah Peeler, have inspired me to think more holistically about the Bible as part of life.

Most notably, my wife Samjung has always sought to help me be the best person I could be, and it is a pleasure to share with her a life that includes our two adult children, Nathan and Hannah. Nathan read this volume and made many insightful comments that sharpened its arguments. This book is dedicated to my family, but no dedication can do justice to the debt I owe them. The ledger will never be balanced in this life, I fear. But perhaps the long-running deficit can remind us that no one lives alone.

1. Robert Penn Warren, *Talking with Robert Penn Warren*, ed. Floyd Watkins, John Hiers, and Mary Louise Weaks (Athens: University of Georgia Press, 1990), 370.

# 1

# Hearing the Bible Afresh

How do we speak of the spiritual dimension of the Bible? It is much like talking about the wetness of water or the automobile-ness of a Bugatti. It seems redundant. After all, the Bible is full of prayers, wise sayings, stories of exemplars and antiheroes, in short, of all the raw materials of a grammar of assent to the presence of God. The best and most obvious place to begin would be the Psalter, that magnificent collection of 150 laments, hymns, wisdom meditations, and so on scanning the spectrum of human emotions from anger to zaniness—or if not that, then at least delirious joy. In these ancient songs, we see shiny bits and pieces of the human encounter with God, all of them merging together in a gorgeous mosaic of faith.

And what a faith! The basic conviction of the Psalter, and indeed of all the Bible, is that the race before us is not too long, nor the foes besetting us too fearsome, nor our own strength too small that we cannot finish with success. Evil does not win, despite all appearances. This is so because we tread the path laid out by the one who accompanies us through the valley of gloom, the God who created the cosmos and from time to time shakes it up a bit so as to leave Mount Zion secure and its citizens confident.

Perhaps a way to begin to understand the Psalms' sense of the presence of God is to notice how the various psalms themselves begin. It is never, of course, easy to begin a poem. I am often glad that I have been given a way to start prayers, "Dear God" or "Our Father in Heaven," so that I didn't have to think of one.

The beginnings of the various psalms say something about their spirituality: "blessed is the one"; "Why do the heathen rage?"; "Oh Lord, how numerous are my enemies!"; "When I call, answer me"; "Hear my utterances O Lord"; "O Lord, in your anger do not rebuke me"; "O Lord our God, how majestic is your name in all the land"; "I will praise the Lord with my whole heart"; "Why, O Lord, do you stand far away?" Those are the first ten entry points in the book of Psalms. We could go on: "O Lord, I called you; notice me"; "I cry with my voice to the Lord"; "O Lord, hear my prayer, listen to my petition"; "blessed be the Lord my rock"; "I shall exalt you, my God the King"; "oh my soul, praise the Lord"; "for it is good to praise our God"; "praise the Lord from the heavens"; "sing to the Lord a new song"; and "praise God in his sanctuary." Those are the last ten. In between the Psalter moves those praying it from the desolation of life seemingly without God to ecstasy—all without escapism or sentimentalism or the life-denying pseudo-piety that so often passes for spirituality in our own time. The Psalms are a nonsense-free zone. They acknowledge human suffering, whether originating in human evil or simply confronting us from nature itself.

But they can look life squarely in the eye because they can see around the corner. The beginning of an honest piety leads us not to despair or cynicism but to hope. Consider just two examples. The forty-sixth psalm boldly opens with an appeal to "our God a refuge and strength in crisis, found strongly to be a help during distress"—or as the King James Version of 1611 puts it so eloquently, "a very present help in trouble." It then offers a way of whistling through the graveyard: "therefore we shall not fear when the earth quakes or the mountains shake in the heart of the seas."

Why such confidence, if it is confidence? Or perhaps better, what spiritual values would lead one to think that perhaps we could steel ourselves in the face of adversity by appealing to God? The Psalmist answers the unspoken question with a warrant for such faith: "There is a river whose streams make God's city rejoice, the holy dwellings of the Most High. God is in its midst. It will not be shaken." The old poetic idea that a river flows through the heavenly mountain of God gets transferred to Zion—where the only rivers exist in the imagination—so that it can be surpassed as a symbol by that to which the symbol points: God's presence. And how does the one praying know when God is present, other than the gorgeous words sung by a believing community? The psalmist answers "Go"—masculine plural—"observe the wonders of the Lord where he has done shocking things in the earth, stopping wars to the ends of the earth, snapping the bow and shattering the spear, torching carts." According to the psalm, what evidence is there that God is present? We can answer that in one word—peace.

The spirituality of the Psalms thus does not land in the calmness of the individual human soul, but in the trust of a community seeking the end of adversity, not just for itself, but for the "ends of the earth." The Psalms of the sons of Korah, of which this is one, long for a resolution of conflict, a worldwide calmness and condition of human wholeness. Thus we read in another one from after the Exile, Psalm 85,

> Oh LORD, you have rescued your land,
>> you have reversed the reversals of Jacob.
> You have removed the iniquity of your people;
>> you have covered all their sins.

It then makes a most interesting move. It says, "Return us O God of our salvation." Which is it? Has God returned us, or must that occur sometime in the future? Or perhaps the juxtaposition of time here—past and future—highlights a present, and indeed abiding reality. In all new situations, we continue to need God's help because we are in danger.

Now you might criticize the psalm's understanding of the world, and any good modern person would raise questions. Doesn't the spirituality of dependence diminish the autonomy and integrity of the human person? Isn't it a form of escapism masquerading as piety, or even worse, a method for evading accountable action in the real world? The answer, I think, is no. No, because claims of human perfectibility lack supporting evidence from our experience or history. No, because the peace sought in the Psalms never comes without a prior commitment to justice. No, because the dream of God's presence does not repeal human dignity but rather consummates it. Thus, the psalm continues a few lines later:

> How near is his rescue to those in awe of him,
>     for his glory to dwell in our land.
> Mercy and trustworthiness meet,
>     justice and peace kiss.
> Trustworthiness springs up from the ground,
>     and justice bends down from heaven.
> Yes, the LORD gives what is good,
>     and our land gives its produce.
> Justice goes forth before him
>     and plants its footsteps on the trail.

The dream of this psalm, and of all the psalms, is not mere personal fulfillment. Our spirituality does not consist of warm moments of personal satisfaction nor the comfort of those who love us nor a sense that all we do is right. After all, such things do the pagans seek.

Beginnings and endings and middles thus give us clues to the spirituality of the Psalms. The vision of the individual praying with a community of people united across the barriers of time and space by a commitment to the creator and judge of the universe surely compels us. But there is one more feature of the spirituality of the Psalms and the Bible as a whole that we must address. It is not a quiet, passive, sweetness-and-light approach to God. Sometimes quarrels break out between God and Israel. Sometimes prophets persuade God to change God's mind. The praying community as a whole speaks openly of God's absence and on occasion of God's unreliability. Sometimes God's presence is experienced as anger, which was the ancient way of describing God's radical commitment to the right. (There are things about which we should be angry!)

Interpreters of these texts have long struggled with how to make sense of such ideas because they seem to be too dynamic and "hot." The wire is a bit too live.

So what should we do with such a querulous and argumentative spirituality? As will become clear below, the Psalms, like the entire Bible in fact, express the deepest human longings so fittingly that it makes sense to introduce them not merely as our words but in some sense, God's. Our longing for God and thus for each other mirrors God's creative work in the cosmos, which seems to express God's movement toward beauty, radical variety, and fruitfulness. Such goals cannot be reached by timid, Hummel-figurine, weak tea and vanilla cookie sorts of prayers. God is not so distant or threatening or, alternatively, given to cheap grace that we must resort to platitudes and clichés in our approach. We need not hide or pretend or pile up approved words and phrases because the spirituality displayed in the Bible does not confine its horizon to the human mind or even human society. Rather, it opens the door to a vision of the world in which, despite our questioning or perhaps because of it, we ask with childlike eagerness, in the words of the hymn: "All things praise thee. Lord, may we?"

## A Prayer

God, it may be true that all things praise you,
> The birds and whales with melodies we admire but cannot imitate,
> The rocks by their epochal steadfastness,
> The flowers by their willingness to bloom for a moment—
> But for us praise does not come easy.
Sometimes we begrudge it, preferring lament and calling to account,
> Sometimes we merely hoard it for ourselves, seeing you as a fierce competitor, and
> Sometimes we merely forget, absorbed by other things.

So even in our forgetting, our grasping, our complaining, let us praise you by being.

For our life comes from you and returns to you and abides in you. Amen.

# 2

# "I am the LORD," or What's in a Name?

*Then God said to Moses, saying, "I am YHWH. I appeared to Abraham, Isaac, and Jacob as El Shaddai but was not known to them by my name YHWH. Moreover, I maintained my covenant with them, to give them the land of Canaan, the land of their migrations through which they migrated. Also, I heard the children of Israel's groaning as Egypt enslaved them, and I remembered my covenant. Therefore, say to the children of Israel, 'I am the Lord, and I will bring you out from Egyptian bondage, and I will rescue you from their enslavement and I will redeem you by an outstretched arm and great judgments. And I will take you to myself as a people, and I will be your God, and you will know that I am the LORD your God, the one bringing you from Egyptian bondage. Then I will bring you to the land that I promised to give to Abraham, Isaac, and Jacob. So I will give it to you as a possession. I am the Lord.'" So Moses said this to Israel's children, but they did not listen to Moses because of their crushed spirit and hard enslavement.*

*Then the LORD said to Moses, "Go, speak to Pharaoh king of Egypt so that he will send forth Israel's children from his land." But Moses replied, "Truly, Israel's children*

*have not listened to me, so how will Pharaoh listen to me?*
*I am a man of uncircumcised lips."*

*The Lord spoke to Moses and to Aaron and com-*
*manded them to go to Pharaoh king of Egypt and instruct*
*him to send forth the children of Israel from the land of*
*Egypt.* (Exodus 6:2–13)

"I don't want to hear it." These are words that we often use in response to bad news. Your job is in jeopardy. I don't want to hear it. You might have cancer. I don't want to hear it. Your children aren't living up to their potential. I don't want to hear it. Don't make me listen.

It is easy to understand why we say this sort of thing to bad news. We hope that if we stop up our ears long enough, maybe the hard truths will go away, and somehow, magically, things will work out differently. "I don't want to hear it" means "the truth hurts, and I can't bear it right now."

What happens, however, when the true word that we don't want to hear is good news? This is the case in our text today, as the people of Israel find themselves unable to bear a word of promise from a loving God spoken by a courageous prophet. No matter how sweet the words, how life-changing the promise, how beautiful the vision, they are unable to listen to a new picture of reality, not because the change it calls for will harm them, but because it will make their lives far better. Yet it will be change, and even the most wonderful change disrupts our patterns of life and forces us to see the contradictions in our viewpoints. Change is always painful, no matter how noble the goal, and so it is with Israel. And besides, they find unbelievable the words of this strange prophet Moses, who has just come in from the desert and failed to persuade Pharaoh of the authority of this new God he proclaims. "Why should we listen to him?" they say. "Beautiful as his words are, they can't be true. And if they are not true, then they are the cruelest things we could hear since they raise hopes impossible to fulfill." And so they did not, and could not, listen. I don't want to hear it!

~

This text comes to us as the conclusion of the first major section of
the book of Exodus, the story of Israel's deliverance from Egyptian
slavery and from the darkness of oppression that enslaves not just
the body, but also the mind and the spirit. In this first part of the
book, chapters 1–6, we hear about a people who must discover
their own name and therefore their own identity. This is why the
book opens with the sentence, "These are the names of the children
of Israel" and then returns in chapter 6 with another list of names
(actually, the same names). The book wants us to have in our heads
a mental map of the people of Israel, assigning to them their proper
designations. And so we hear of Amram and Jochebed the parents,
Shiphrah and Puah the midwives, Miriam and Aaron and Zipporah and Gershom and Eliezer. And we emphatically do not hear of
the names of the Pharaoh and his henchmen, all of whom remain
anonymous, as though the book of Exodus wants to remind us that
in God's world, those who would strip away the dignity of other
human beings risk losing their own identity as well.

Most of all, we hear the name of the Lord, Yahweh, the God of
Israel and of the whole Universe, the creator and promise-keeper,
the sustainer of goodness and enemy of evil. We hear this name
revealed at Mount Horeb or Sinai from the flames of a burning
bush, as Yahweh says back in chapters 3 and 4, "I am who I am . . .
I am the God of Abraham, Isaac, and Jacob." Now Moses, go. Go
and announce the coming deliverance. Go and tell of a new world.
Go and speak this world into being.

But of course worlds don't just appear because we wish them
to. Moses' first action back in Egypt, forty years after he immigrat-
ed to Midian, was to demand the release of the Israelite captives.
This demand fell on deaf ears. Or rather not deaf exactly, but ears
and eyes carefully protected from detecting justice and fairness
and common decency. He spoke to Pharaoh, a man whose view
of the world centered on the idea that some people—his people,
and he most of all—were born to rule, while others were born to
be ruled. Ruled like so many animals. And Moses' cry for common

decency had met only greater oppression. So in despair, he comes back to the Lord and says, in effect, "This mission you have sent me on is a failure. I do not know what to do now."

This is where we are in today's text. And in some ways perhaps it is where we find ourselves in our own lives and in the church's collective life. For like Moses, we may have tried to do something about the wrong in the world only to find that our intervention failed or even backfired. What are we to do? At just this point, God goes to work, and our text becomes most instructive.

∼

In order to encourage Moses to continue with his work, God does at least two things. The more important is that he reminds Moses of the story of God and Israel, both past and future. And so we hear the Lord saying twelve things about himself:

- I appeared to Abraham, Isaac, and Jacob

- I made a covenant with them to give them the land of Canaan

- I heard the groaning of their descendants, the slaves in Egypt

- I remembered my covenant

- I will deliver Israel as I promised

- I will rescue you from your slavery

- I will redeem you with an outstretched arm

- I will be your God

- You will know that I am your God when I bring you out of bondage

- I will bring you to Canaan

- I will do this because I promised Abraham, Isaac, and Jacob that I would

- I will give it to you

Appeared. Heard. Remembered. Acted and is acting and will continue to act to save and redeem. These are the twelve ways in which God is revealed to Moses and, through him, to all the people of Israel and in due time to all of us. Here we see a God who does not merely sit up in heaven and observe human behavior like a brilliant scientist studying ants or lab rats. No, here is a God who interacts with human beings to their benefit. This God builds long-term relationships with entire communities of people, connecting ancestors to descendants in a web of promises kept and dreams lived out. This is a God who calls upon all of us to live with justice toward each other as we protect and uplift the weakest among us. And most of all, this is a God who defeats the powers of evil so that goodness may prevail.

And so God speaks to Moses first of all about the story into which he, the reluctant prophet leading a reluctant people, is entering. Now, if you think about it, all of us live out a story in our lives. People don't answer "who are you?" with just dry facts, much less abstract attributes such as "I am male, mortal, ignorant of some things and knowledgeable about others." And in the same way, God does not say, "Remember that I am immortal, infinite, all-knowing, and omnipresent." No. If the Bible is to be believed, both we and God introduce ourselves through telling our stories, and fortunately for us, God's story is really a story about us as we stand before God.

And so it is true here in Exodus. The Lord says to Moses that it makes sense to carry on with the difficult mission of speaking truth to power, of doing the right thing for the right reasons even when we face opposition, even when the opposition comes from those who should welcome the mission. It makes sense to carry on because the mission is part of the great story of trust in the promises of God stretching back over generations and across many kilometers.

So what is the story into which God brings Israel and all who follow in their footsteps? Or to put it another way, in any story, there are characters (people who do things), a plot (things that happen in a certain order), and a setting in which the story happens. There are heroes and villains, actions and failures to act. Things happen in any story. So what happens in God's story?

The answer to this question is that throughout the Bible and throughout the church's life across the centuries, God has been at work not only to forgive and heal human sin but also to remove the pain of human suffering in anticipation of the day when every tear will be wiped from every eye. God has invited people into the work of telling the truth in love so that true justice and peace may become a reality. As the great German martyr Dietrich Bonhoeffer put it, "No peace is peace but that which comes through the forgiveness of sins." And to this we might add, not just through the forgiveness of sins but through the healing of the victims of sin.

This is part of God's story among human beings. As Christians, we believe that God hears every cry of every suffering person. We also believe that God has called us Christians to serve the sick, the dying, the poor, and the mistreated without asking for anything for ourselves in return. As God has blessed us, so we try to bless others. And even with all our flaws and failures, the church has a long history of being just such people. We try to live out a story in which the liberated slaves are freed to be full human beings before God, so that they also can serve in freedom out of love, not in bondage out of fear. This is the church's story, and it was the one God began with Abraham and Sarah and all the rest.

Now there is also a second thing that God does here in this story that we need to hear about. And that is that when Moses complains and states that the vision of hope is impossible to realize, God simply reminds him of the larger truth of salvation. He does not allow Moses to wallow in self-pity or to give up when the road gets hard. Nor does God scold Moses or try to shame him into doing the right thing. Rather, God does a very simple thing that has great power: he reminds Moses that the deliverance of the people does not depend upon the wisdom or strength of any human being, including Moses himself. Deliverance is an act of God's grace—unmerited, undeserved, immeasurable in its effects.

I think this is a point that deserves our attention today because it is easy for us to grow frustrated or weary when we don't see the world going the way we think it should. This is especially true if we are accustomed to the church growing and rising from one success to another. When the things we have done successfully in the past suddenly stop working, or when we see moral or spiritual failure, or when there is just a spiritual sleepiness all around us—at those times it is easy to become desperate, to look about for something or someone to blame, or maybe just to try to hide from reality. Self-pity is a real danger, especially for those of us called upon to lead the church in its mission.

But in this story, God says to Moses, "Look, we are in the business of rewriting the story of this people. They believe that the world is cruel and their fate is hopeless. They believe that God is indifferent. But that is not the true story. We must help them hear something else. We must speak to them of hope, for that is the true story of human existence."

In the spring of 2015, I had the opportunity to teach biblical studies at a number of Korean universities with people from several Christian traditions. These men and women from Korea and a dozen other countries share in common a great love for God and a great trust in the hopefulness of the Gospel.

One of my students in Korea came from Myanmar, where she works with refugees in the camps to which they have fled from the military government of their own country. She says, "They want to know why this has happened to them and whether God cares." "What do you tell them?" I ask. "That I don't know why or even if there is a why, but that I believe that God does care and continues to hear their prayers." That conviction takes faith, but it is the central belief of us Christians, as well as the very thing to which God called Moses, and through him, Israel and all the rest of us.

Another of my students from Myanmar speaks of how the people he knows have "dark minds." I have come to appreciate that expression in part because it describes the situation in Exodus as well. Their suffering, the ways in which they have borne the weight of other people's sins, has stripped them of their hope. They struggle to believe that anything else is possible. And so he studies here in Korea, this great country, to prepare to go home so that he can bring light to those same minds. Being with Christians here has made a difference for him, just as it has for me. And for this we are grateful.

~

So dark minds and broken hearts lie all around us. We know this. But there is a greater truth that we also know : that we can act. The story of our lives does not end in tragedy because our story is part of a larger one, the greatest story of all, the one whose author sits on the throne of heaven and descends to a cross. And in this story we also can act.

And so this day, now, let us resolve that we too shall hear and remember and act. Let us feed the hungry and visit the prisoners. Let us bring knowledge where ignorance reigns, and joy where sorrow prevails. And above all, let us hear and speak the healing words uttered long ago, "I am the Lord." For in knowing that name lies the hope of us all.

## A Prayer

O God, the final "amen" will be the easiest because by then our affirmations will be indistinguishable from our gaze upon you as we enjoy your company forever. Until then, our "amens" mean "we will try to trust" or "we hope this is right" or "let's see if this works."

O God, the final "amen" will come not from our closets where we pray in trust, but from a cosmic assembly around the heavenly throne. Until then, hear our lone mutterings, our whispers, our cries.

O God, the final "amen"—but there is no final one, only an ever-growing chorus that sings, as John the Prophet taught Handel the composer, "Worthy is the lamb." Indeed. Amen.

# 3

## Connecting the Dots

*Blessed is the one who does not frequent the meetings of the*
  *wicked*
*nor stand on the path of sinners*
  *nor sit down with scoffers.*
*That person enjoys YHWH's Torah and*
  *Mulls over that Torah day and night.*
*So he or she is like a tree planted beside irrigation canals,*
  *Giving its fruit at the right time*
  *With unwithered leaves.*
*Everything that one does prospers.*

*Not so the wicked ones!*
  *No, they are like the chaff that the wind whisks away.*
*So, the wicked ones do not stand up in court,*
  *Nor the sinners in the meetings of the righteous.*
*For YHWH knows the path of the righteous ones,*
  *but the path of the wicked ones dies off.* (Psalm 1)

Piety. Wisdom. Pleasure. The first Psalm puts these words together, strangely. I say strangely because we rarely do. They seem, frankly, to operate in different worlds. The first is a little old-fashioned and,

17

what's worse, stuffy. The second is desirable if it doesn't cost too much or insist too ardently on a change in behavior. The third is easiest, though in all honesty, we've had enough of the narcissism of other people, even if we wish to indulge our own narcissism just a bit longer. Perhaps we can combine any two: a wise person might be deeply religious, like Moses or the Dalai Lama; pleasure can be redefined as self-actualization, and in some ethical systems at least (such as the American cult of pragmatic libertarianism) being your best self is the highest attainable wisdom; but combining piety and pleasure may require a suppression of too many desires or just too much plain weirdness to be appealing.

It's hard enough with two, but all three?

You can see the difficulty with a very simple experiment. Try Googling images of each word. The first gets you pictures of Luther standing before the cross or families praying or an Indian yogi sitting in the lotus position. The second draws up wisdom teeth, Buddha, Einstein, fortune cookies, and, of all people, Clint Eastwood. The third—well, you don't need me to tell you what the third query yields. The differences must reflect our modern trifurcation of soul, mind, and body with our culture's strong preference for the last.

Yet things have not always been so, and for the psalmist, the split personality does not exist. Right-thinking and vital people can take pleasure in the deepest intellectual and spiritual pursuits because they merge into one another. We don't have to be an Aristotle, who thought that God, as the perfectly happy and perfect unified being, would contemplate only Godself and thus would draw the wise into such contemplation, to recognize that there may be a way to draw together these three words by rethinking what each means. We only need to recognize that the highest beatitude of the human being is not self-actualization, much less the pursuit of transient social or material goods, but the quest for our truest selves in the presence of the Good, the True, and the Beautiful—all with capital letters, and all shorthand for the source of all, namely God. The wisdom to strip away from our lives all the things that mar God's image in us, the piety to bring both strengths and weaknesses to the Healer and Redeemer of us all, and the pleasure that comes from putting our center in our middle—all these things converge.

So hear what the Psalmist says, and hear what the collectors of the Psalter as a whole thought should be the image of the ideal human being. He or she chooses associates wisely and does not engage in the business of injustice wherever it is practiced. He or she contemplates the Law of the Lord day and night, obsessively as it were.

This last part is most interesting to me, and I hope to us of all as a community of teachers and learners. What does it mean to delight in Torah and contemplate it all the time? In our world of terabytes of trivia and mountains of minutiae, how can anyone immerse herself in so small an ocean as a single book?

The answer is that the world behind the book is God's world and is therefore a cosmos. It is a world of dreams and visions, of storytellers and poets, wonder-working seers speaking oracles summoning the powerful to service and the servants to power. It is a world in which donkeys speak and whales obey, in which carpenters walk on water and, far more astonishingly, prophets invite sexually parlous women to drink living water and righteous priests to be born again. It is a world that begins in a garden and ends in a paradise, each place graced by marvelous trees for the healing of the nations.

In short, it is the real world, not our world of gray shadows and failed promises, of hidden agendas and not so hidden maneuvers. Torah teaches us about sublimity, and thus about our need for transcendence. No wonder the psalmist celebrates the persons who dare to inhabit it!

Now I know that this all sounds quite paradoxical. But the truth always does because we have grown so accustomed to cheap knock-offs of it. As Dryden put it, "There is a pleasure sure / In being mad which none but madmen know." All of us know it, and we build our economy and our governments and even our churches on the congenital madness of the human race, which we used to call original sin but now call "being human." Yet it is also true that few of us are completely mad, and most of us seek sanity, hence our contemplation of the divine and our search to link together the qualities of life—piety, wisdom, and pleasure—that our madness has separated.

How do we proceed? You are where you are today because, like the Psalmist, you want to learn to escape the counsels of the wicked and be life-bearing like gorgeous plants in a garden. You are where you are today because you are ready to think deeply, not only about your chosen profession, whatever it is, but about the deepest questions that we humans can ask. You are where you are today because you wish to challenge the easy assumptions you have acquired and to seek not appearances, but truth. And you are where you are because you believe that quest involves God and humanity, somehow united.

How do we proceed? One of my favorite American poets, Wendell Berry, once saw some pictures in a magazine, maybe the *National Geographic*, of a Siberian woodsman. This was during the Cold War when humans decided that it was rational to acquire the ability to obliterate the biosphere. Better the cockroaches should win than that the other side should! So Berry writes against the madness:

> There is no government so worthy as your son who fishes
> with you in silence beside the forest pool.
> There is no national glory so comely as your daughter
> whose hands have learned a music and go their own
> way on the keys.
> There is no national glory so comely as my daughter who
> dances and sings and is the brightness of my house.
> There is no government so worthy as my son who
> laughs, as he comes up the path from the river in the
> evening, for joy.[1]

Surely the insight comes directly from Torah and is the most biblical and Christian thing in the world.

1. Wendell Berry, "To a Siberian Woodsman," in *Collected Poems 1957–1982* (New York: Farrar, Straus & Giroux, 1984), 98.

So today, go forth and be sane. Love God's world, and love God. Dream and toil, laugh and cry, learn and teach, and be. Blessed are you. Blessed are you.

## A Prayer

Lord, hear our cry like a newborn's first gasp for air,
    Like a dying woman's struggle for breath,
    Like a drowning man thrashing about for oxygen.
    So is our need to speak to you.
Lord, see our tears like a people defeated by their foes,
    Like a child losing a beloved grandfather,
    Like a husband and wife who can never give birth.
    So is our need to speak to you.
Lord, join our song like a funeral congregation's "Amazing Grace,"
    Like "Taps" for the last doughboy,
    Like "Blest be the Tie" from grandmother's coming and
        going mind.
    So is our need to speak to you.
And so is our need to hear you speak back. Amen.

# 4

## Stumbling toward Escape

*Why do the nations fume*
*    and the peoples scheme stupidly?*
*Earth's kings stand up, yet rulers set themselves together,*
*    Against Yhwh and his anointed one.*
*"Let us smash their chains*
*    and throw their fetters off ourselves," they say.*
*The one sitting in the Heavens laughs.*
*The Lord mocks them,*
*    says to them angrily, threatens them wrathfully:*
*"I have set my king on Zion, my holy mount."*

*Let me recount Yhwh's decree,*
*He said to me, "You are my son.*
*    Today I give you birth.*
*Ask me and I will make the nations your property,*
*    the ends of the earth your estate."*
*He will smash them with an iron rod,*
*    shatter them like so many clay pots.*
*So now, kings, be smart.*
*    Learn the lesson, earth's judges.*

*Serve Y*HWH *with awe and celebrate dominion.*
*Kiss the son lest he be upset*
    *and you perish on the road.*
*Though his anger burns awhile,*
    *blessed are those who trust in him.* (Psalm 2)

There is trouble in the world. Mind-bending, heart-rending trouble. The noise of seven billion human beings striving, hunting, sweating, toiling, longing, losing—and winning for the moment, but only for the moment—fills the earth that once was silent and still. Every September we face the anniversary of that fateful day in 2001 when our illusions of safety and meaning, the end of history, died with the impact of jumbo jets on cold glass and steel. The ghosts of past sins interrupted our dreams of weal. Buildings collapsed and hopes with them. But then, even that was only a moment in the vast sweep of the human history of tragedy and dark comedy as our race, on its millennia-long march of folly, slouches toward its final Gomorrah. Why do the nations rage? Because there is nothing else we can do but rage and plot. Oh, there is trouble in the world. Mind-bending, heart-rending trouble. And its name is humankind.

Our psalmist tried to capture the trouble of the world with the disjointed language of voices coming and going, the nations, the king of Jerusalem, and most notably and confoundingly God. Psalm 2 is a very noisy text with posturing and strident tones, a "come and get me" sort of approach that would have made Shakespeare's Henry V proud. "We would not die in that man's company that fears his fellowship to die with us." And through it all, the psalm signals the pointlessness of our politics and commerce, the patterns of rivalry and contestation that shape almost every corner of our being. The deep human desire to be free of the shackles of obedience to God comes to the surface here, albeit in the language of political struggle. And the psalm tells us something deeply true about ourselves, namely that our strife continues because we wish it so. If we wish it to stop, we must ask why willing its end is so difficult.

The great artists, poets, and theologians have always taught us this. The psalmist knows this sentiment too because he or she ends with a simple cry out of the din: "blessed are all who trust in him." It sounds at first like a throwaway line, a statement of resignation amid the unstoppable cacophony of life or even worse, the hopelessly sentimental piety of the overly timid. But the observation, the beatitude, does not state a vain wish, nor is it escapist or sanctimonious. Not at all. Rather, Psalm 2 closes with a theme that opened Psalm 1, the possibility of solace and the necessity of choice. For it is only in the choice to seek the way that delights in God's communication with us that we can find the quietness of soul that allows us to survive the inescapable trouble around us.

Today, we invite each other to find a quiet place far from the noise. We repeat God's invitation to hear amidst the clanging, clattering clamor of the world a different music. The world we have created reports to us the conflicts within ourselves, the divided consciousness, the torn soul. We hear often of the tensions between mind and heart, between rigorous pursuit of knowledge and vigorously loving service. We must choose, the strident voices tell us, between our hands and our hearts, our minds and our souls, as though these are not all God's gifts to us, as though God were powerful or good or imaginative enough to redeem only a part of us. But it is not so. The clatter does not, after all, arise solely outside of us. It also lives within.

And so, knowing all this, the psalm invites us, just as we invite each other, to another reality, one in which the harmonies of the angels play even beneath the crash and tumult of human existence. But you know, there is a curious thing here, or rather two curious things. One is that the symphony of heaven, the song of the soul that speaks the truth about our longings and laments can draw into itself even the stray noises of life and turn them into something beautiful so that nothing is really wasted or lost. The second is more wonderful still. It is the reality that the God who sets a king on Zion and smashes the foes of peace can also gather the shards of our lives and mend them together into beautiful vessels, Ming vases from the bits and pieces of our existence. This is the great miracle of grace. No wonder the psalm ends with "blessed are those who trust in God."

So yes, there is trouble in the world. Mind-bending, heart-rending trouble. But behind it, in front of it, even within it lies something else, or rather some*one* else. Today, let us cast our cares on the God who cares for us, for in God's hands we are free to be ourselves, free to be broken yet mending, beginning and ending, uniting our whole being into one before the God who made us and loves us more than we can love ourselves. Let us be calm of soul so that we may act with boldness, think with clarity, love with solidarity, so live our lives that when the end comes we may truly say that we have trusted in God's melodious offer of grace with all our hearts. Blessed are all of you who trust in God, to whom be glory in Christ Jesus, world without end.

## A Prayer

O God, do not laugh at our troubles, for even a chuckle sends us over the edge.
Weep with us at the terrorist's knife,
    At the state's smart bombs and smart people,
    At the daily crushing of spirits for the world's fuel.
O God, do not laugh at our troubles, for every grin drives in us a wedge.
Weep with us for the girls sold for sex,
    For the boys armed with AK-47s,
    For the mothers and fathers torn apart.
O God, why do the nations fume? And why do we sit by idly laughing when you fume too? Amen.

# 5

## Out of the Mouth of Infants

*For the choirmaster to the tune "Gittith." A psalm for David.*
*Y*HWH*, our Lord,*
    *how noble is your name throughout the earth.*
*Who has put your glory in the heavens?*
    *From the unweaned babies' mouths,*
*you mount up the strength,*
    *In response to your foes, to stop the enemy and the vengeful.*
*When I scan your heavens, your fingers' work,*
    *The moon and the stars that you fashioned—*
*What is a human being that deserves your memory*
    *Or a homo sapiens that you should pay attention to it?*
*You made them just less than the divine beings,*
    *Crowned them with glorious splendor.*
*You made them ruler over your hands' works,*
    *Put everything under their feet.*
*All the flocks and herds, yes, the untamed beasts,*
    *The birds in the sky and the fish in the sea,*
    *Those crossing the oceans' depths.*
*Y*HWH *our Lord,*
    *how noble is your name in all the earth!* (Psalm 8)

"O LORD, our Lord, how noble is your name in all the earth." The Bible is a very surprising book. The more you read it, the more surprising it is. And few texts are more astonishing than the eighth psalm as it celebrates the stunning beauty and dignity of creation, including humankind.

Consider the line "out of the mouth of babes and infants you have established strength." If we forget for a moment the sentimentality that surrounds very small children—the infants and babes—we realize that in fact they are deeply troubling beings. They are untidy in their persons and surroundings. Sloppy eaters. They smell bad, and they hardly ever make deadlines. Thanks to the invention of disposable diapers, they are a major factor in the pollution of the planet. You can never consult them for advice on your love life. Hardly the place to go when you want to build a foundation for anything, much less something as significant as God's plan for defeating enemies, whoever they are.

Of course, the psalmist knows that, and like the other composers of psalms in our Bible, he or she is nobody's fool and not given to sentimentality. The psalmist knows very well that there is a still darker side, not to children but to the lives that some of them must lead. Indeed, most of the time when you see this pair, "babes and infants," in the Old Testament it's in the context of warfare. "Babes and infants" cry out in pain as the invaders pour over the city walls. Children, the aged, and the sick are the victims of invasion, famine, drought, and disease. While some ride in their SUVs from soccer game to piano lessons to gymnastics, with a quick stop at Pizza Hut thrown in, other children live different lives.

"Different lives" means that this year, according to the CIA's World Factbook, as many as 115 of a thousand children born in Afghanistan will not see their first birthday. In the United States, the number is about six. The psalmist would not be surprised—though still dismayed as we no longer are—to see on the television news the pictures of ten-year-old boys toting guns in a civil war. Or to hear of the children who live in the tombs around Cairo, or their brothers and sisters who pick through the trash in Manila. Or the children of New York and Dallas and Abilene whose parents cannot both feed them and provide them with medicine. And for the ancient Israelites, these would not be mere statistics but flesh and blood and bone and fat. Humankind. "What is a human being that deserves your memory, or a homo sapiens that you should pay attention to it?"

As I say, the psalmist is not blind to all this. Surely the condition of children is proof enough that humankind is seriously flawed. So why talk so oddly about babes and infants? Because there is another possibility, another vision. People of faith recognize that God has not given over his world to the warlords and the billionaires. The powers that be will fade away—even the world's last remaining superpower. To express this alternative vision, the psalm uses the language of divine warfare, language that began with the mythologies of the ancient Near East but in Israel came to be not about God's fight with a sea monster, but his triumph over men and women, Pharaoh and Jezebel, who use their power and wealth only to accumulate more. The message of Scripture is that God will tear apart stone by stone the walls of fear and prejudice that diminish human dignity. And with the power of love, unchoked by pride, God will overwhelm his enemies by restoring to them and to us all the true depths of dignity he intended for us originally.

Nor is this all. In his book *Ordinary Resurrections*, Jonathan Kozol tells the story of Stephanie, a young girl from a poor neighborhood in the South Bronx. Raised by her single mother, she longs for security and safety. In response to Kozol's question of what would make the world a better place, she says, "What would make the world better is God's heart . . . I know God's heart is already in the world. But I would like it if he would . . . push the heart more into it. Not just halfway. Push it more!"[1]

It's a naïve way of putting it, corny almost. But still, that's the vision. The psalmist sees it too. Humankind fills all the ecosystems ancient people know about—land, sky, and sea. And we engage all of creation responsibly, recognizing that our actions

---

1. Jonathan Kozol, *Ordinary Resurrections: Children in the Years of Hope* (New York: Crown, 2000), 72.

have consequences. We are responsible, as all entrusted with rule and crowned with glory and honor have to be. And the dignity of humankind is not just a set of empty platitudes, but a living, breathing reality that informs all we think and do and care about.

So the vision is more than just an idle dream, a vague pleasant-sounding utopia we can talk about in the comfort of our churches. It is a challenge too, a clarion call to care, to work, to sweat, to sacrifice, to make a difference. And it is our call as people, Jews and Christians and others, who take seriously the words of this psalm.

Let us see this vision. In those quiet moments when we are alone with God and ourselves, let us dream of a world in which no children go hungry or are beaten or ignored. Let us commit our lives and talents and skills to the realization of this vision. Let us dream of building this new reality, realizing this glorious vision, embracing this tomorrow of the soul. For then the words of Jesus will no longer be just words, but the way things are: "Let the children come to me." And as we in awe whisper to each other, "What is humanity that you are mindful of him," we hear from the mouths of the littlest of us, we hear the grace-filled words, "O LORD, our Lord, how majestic is your name in all the earth."

## A Prayer

In the beginning, O Lord, you said, "Let light be," and light was. You continue to give light in dark places so that all your creation may see you as you truly are, not in shadows or by faint hints, but in the utmost clarity. You give light so that we need not be afraid to allow our lives to be seen by others.

Make us, O God, the light of the world, a city set on a hill, not hidden, but a place of refuge for the innocent who seek you.

Shine on us, O Christ, so that we may awaken from our sleep and may cast off the stupor brought on by our shame or greed or indifference so that we may be truly awake.

Descend on us, O Holy Spirit, so that your fire may allow our tongues to speak words of hope and reconciliation.

Our God, most gracious Father, Son, and Spirit, those who sit in darkness have seen a great light. Open our eyes so that we may see your face. Open our ears so that we may hear the cries of your suffering people. Open our hands so that we may act in service. For in your light, we see light. Amen.

# 6

## Urban Dreams

*For the choir director of the Korahite Singers. A song to the tune*
*"Alamoth."*
*God is, for us, a refuge and source of strength;*
  *He is found to be a great help during troubles.*
*Therefore, we will not fear,*
  *though the earth shake or the seamounts quake,*
  *his waters roar, foam, the mountains quiver at his power.*

*The cosmic river's streams gladden God's city,*
  *the holy dwellings of the Most High.*
*God is inside it, so it will not be shaken.*
  *God will help it before morning comes.*
*Nations roar! Kingdoms quaver!*
  *God shouts and the earth trembles.*
*Yhwh Almighty is with us. Jacob's God is our hideaway.*

*Go, gaze upon Yhwh's deeds to earth's ends:*
  *Bows snapped, spears smashed, shields torched.*
*"Stop and know that I am God.*
  *I excel the nations and all the earth."*
*Yhwh Almighty is with us. Jacob's God is our hideaway.*
(Psalm 46)

Cities are fascinating places. London. New York. Seoul. Rome. Jerusalem. (Jerusalem in particular, for that's where I met my wife when we were students together.) Cities intrigue us not just because of the buildings and roads and sewer lines and subways and all the intricate systems that must come together to make them work. Those are fascinating enough. But cities are interesting also because they embody dreams. Sometimes this is obvious, as when Washington was built with broad boulevards connecting monuments right and left. Something similar goes for Brasilia or Canberra or St. Petersburg, or even Paris after Napoleon III got through with it. Cities are ideas. And in this life, ideas matter more than anything else.

And so the psalmist talks about the idea of Jerusalem. For him or her, it was not just a spot on a map or a few hills walled about with a temple tucked away in the northeast corner. In this place God the Almighty creator of everything, the God of peace and justice, enters into human affairs in a very splashy way. The divine drama involves the end of warfare, not just the defeat of Israel's enemies, but the end of all strife. The psalm rises above petty nationalism or the parochial love of family and homeland to a higher plane in which it is possible to dream about a world no human has ever seen—the world in which conflict has ceased.

Or perhaps not quite ceased. That vision of the divine city awaits a much later time, as the book of Revelation makes clear. In this psalm, the city of peace exists as a calm place amid the upheaval of the rest of the world. Literally upheaval, for the psalmist resorts to the language of heavy surf against the rocks as well as earthquake, with its fantastic twisting and tearing of rock and soil. Amid the violent anarchy of a world in which unenlightened self-interest trumps not just altruism but even long-term promises, the city sits in calm. Its citizens walk the streets safely at night. They know their neighbors. They know when and how and why to celebrate. And they do.

Yet the imagery is tricky. Today we see, and some of us live in, gated communities whose inhabitants seem to believe that money can buy security. As long as they can live in comfort and ease without fearing their neighbors, then the rest of the world can go to perdition. As long as their children receive a good education, then the other children can fend for themselves in unsafety. As long as they can find diversion in sex, sports, and sun-filled holidays on sandy beaches, then the fate of those "less fortunate" matters not at all. Or if the last glimmer of conscience rears its head to assert the claims of other humans, then religion can come as a palliative to sedate the last sense of solidarity with the distorted claim that only my relationship to God matters in the end.

This distortion of the idea of God's refuge is far from the psalm's intention, in part because the psalm comes from a moral person living in a moral community. Escape does not happen through accumulation of things or the illusions of security and well-being that they can purchase. The safety of the heavenly city is not for sale.

To be fair, let's recognize that wealthy conservatives haven't cornered the market on delusions of safety. Every Facebook feed on earth, including mine, is an exercise in just this sort of wall-building. This is a human problem, one deeply rooted in our nature. The desire to surround ourselves with like-minded persons and to screen out the "other" comes as a downside of our mostly laudable tendency to draw sustenance from family. (Remember that the old Latin word *familia* gives us "family," "familiar," and dozens of related words since it entered the English language in the 1300s.) We have a biological instinct for the familiar. It's how our species survives. Yet we can over-perform a good thing. The familiar can seem safe even when it is not, even when it creates dangers for everyone around us.

So this psalmist does not seek to build an enclave in which protected people can indulge their fantasies of autonomy and self-worth. No ancient Israelite could long believe in the possibility of such a thing. The world's dangers to this small minority always broke through the illusions.

Instead, the psalm insists on a very clear point. The refuge lies precisely *in God*. "God," the song insists, "is our refuge, a great help during trouble . . . Jacob's God is our hideaway." This psalm reveals a profound, radical trust in God as the one building the city around the idea of peace, the dignity of every human being, the vigorous pursuit of goodness. Yet God is not that city. Love of neighbor and love of God are closely related but not identical— God, not just our ideas about God or our ritual practices or our always fragile morality.

The faith of this psalmist rests on a simple assumption: God can be trusted in an ultimate way, in a way that no other reality can be. Human beings may reasonably attune our entire network of values, commitments, hopes, and loves toward the God whose story with human beings (and Israel in particular) is one of covenant-making and keeping. As the one whose prophets encouraged the exiled Israelites to rebuild Jerusalem and reimagine themselves in it, the God of this psalm can inspire human confidence. The city that God builds does not exist merely as stones and mortar, wood and iron, buildings and streets and plazas and parks. No, this city exists inside the hearts and minds of people, and it takes shape as those people build lives together. The city of God can exist in Mumbai or Memphis, in Shanghai or Schenectady. It does not exist, however, unless human beings engage the idea behind it, of all creation living in harmony with God. The psalm offers, in short, an explicitly religious view of the city.

Today, of course, most human beings live in cities, and we choose where we live. In fact, the right of choice is enshrined in international law and our noblest moral declarations. Yet the city in which we live also needs us to shape it, not just its buildings but its hearts and minds. The idea of the city is the idea of what it means to be human. And that is worth reflecting on.

## A Prayer

Lord of small spaces, obscure, half-forgotten amid the enormity of concrete and steel, you hear the faintest whimper of the broken-hearted amid the pandemonium of Megalopolis. We would like to think that our speedways and alleyways, so full of our life and our death, mean something also to you, though we wonder if we are deceiving ourselves on this point. We forget that the aggregate has interest, even to us, as a sum of its infinity of parts, most minute and unworthy of enumeration, closed to reflection, unseeable even when we stare. And so we pray that you will aid us in thinking small enough to see the enormous. Help us to recognize evil and banality so we may know also what is good. And as we build monuments to our dreams for ourselves, our ideas of how creation ought to run, help us to remember to hear your much larger dreams for us and thereby to discipline our own. Amen.

# 7

## The Lord Reigns, but Am I Glad?

*Hallelujah.*
*Praise Yhwh, my inner self.*
*Let me praise Yhwh by my life,*
   *let me sing to my God by my existence.*
*Do not trust in nobles,*
   *human beings in whom is no salvation.*
*Their spirits go out, returning to the ground.*
   *On that very day, their plans succumb.*

*Blessed is the person whose helper is Jacob's God,*
   *whose hope is in Yhwh his or her God,*
*the one making heaven and earth, the sea and all in them,*
   *the one always reliable.*
*The one defending the oppressed,*
   *feeding the hungry.*
*Yhwh frees the prisoners.*
   *Yhwh gives sight to the blind.*
*Yhwh elevates the prostrate.*
   *Yhwh loves the righteous.*
*Yhwh preserves the immigrants.*

*He helps the orphan and widow,*
*but makes the road of the wicked people crooked.*
*YHWH reigns forever.*
*Zion, your God rules in every generation.*
*Hallelujah.* (Psalm 146)

Well, I get it. The psalmist rejoices in God because God has cared for, you pick them, the downtrodden and the hungry and the prisoners and the blind and the righteous—how did they get in there?—and the immigrants and the widows and the orphans. I get it. The God of the Bible is one who fills the poor with good and sends the rich away empty, as Mary sang after Jesus' birth. The God of the Bible is disgusted by pious religious words that mask immoral lives and is dismayed by chattering prayers that smugly celebrate the good things in the life of the person who prays without caring about the lives of others. The God of the Bible is unimpressed by a type of religious faith, or superstition really, that imagines that God picks people's spouses or jobs or housing developments for them but is indifferent to the suffering of millions. The God of the Bible is one who inspires the prophet Amos to long for the day when "justice will roll down like waters and righteousness like a mighty stream." This is a God who "will reign forever / your God, O Zion, from generation to generation." So, I get it. This is not the God of a large portion of American Christianity. Or perhaps even mine and yours.

I say this for one simple reason, and not just for cheap thrills. Reading a psalm like 146 produces mixed feelings. After all, I'm not one of the poor. I have more than one change of clothes, my pantry is full of food, and my car's gas tank is full of fuel. I am a native of my own land and travel freely and have never had to decide whether to feed my family or obey unjust and hypocritical laws. Any hunger of mine is self-imposed, an attempt to make up for years of excess and waste. What does this psalm have to do with me? Why can't it be more modern and real and accommodating of the prejudices and fears and hopes, however false, of my middle class life?

But there it is. A psalm that joyously praises Israel's God because that God has demonstrated care for the most vulnerable among us and has even equated them, as the Bible does many times, with the righteous. For in many Old Testament texts, the poor and righteous are the same people, or at least the groups overlap far more extensively than we Americans believe. Affluence does not correlate with integrity in any meaningful way.

Still, we bear a moral responsibility to hear this text from its own perspective and from the vantage point of its intended performers, namely, those who would be glad to see God care for the most vulnerable among us. And so I must recognize a few things about the text. Let me name three.

First, let's notice how this psalm proceeds. The psalmist talks to himself or herself, and in this self-talk paints a sharp contrast between the easy trust in human achievement, on the one hand, and the difficult trust in God, on the other. Trust in human achievement, no matter how grand, is ultimately futile because, well, human beings die. And our plans often die with us.

Alas.

Or often, not so much alas because sometimes our plans do not deserve to outlast us. Our lives are circumscribed by the great gulfs of birth and death, which we must cross unencumbered by the many helps we accumulate in life. The psalmist knows, of course, that laziness and unintentionality are not the answers and even that cynicism is a commitment of sorts, if a bad one. And this is why the psalm does not dwell on the ultimate demise of our plans but emphasizes instead the work of God. It describes God as the creator of all and argues that the most fitting thing God does in this creation is to care for all creatures, including the smallest and weakest of us. This is the great truth of the world. Human grandeur is an illusion, but so is our sense of being alone in the cosmos. All of us live in the care of a tender God unless we refuse to accept it.

This is the second thing, then. The psalmist expects his or her hearers to relish the success of the poor. We should not see the world as a place of deprivation and scarcity but as one in which another's victory does not imply my defeat. It is not a zero-sum game. The "other" is not a threat, or at least not automatically so. There is something mind-bending about this idea, of course. The insight that the care of the vulnerable must inform our stance toward the interactions of human beings in the world—our political theory, our votes on economic policy—seems lost on many Christians in America. Hence the brutal stridency of our political discourse, hence the church's horrendous reputation in many circles. How will I move my mind and heart to the place where I am willing to have a little less so that my more vulnerable neighbor can have more? Can I really say "Amen" to good old Mary's prayer when she celebrates the reversal of fortune. Only if I trust in God is that possible.

And so this brings me to the third observation. Psalm 146 is part of a larger unit in the book of Psalms. Psalms 146–50 form a sort of triumphant ending to the whole book. A noisy, raucous ending that celebrates Yahweh's presence among a people who have experienced exile and loss, people who have left their land awhile and now returned to face an uncertain future. Psalm 146 is the beginning of the end, the opening theme in the conclusion. And that theme is that those who pray this psalm may imagine a different future than the present one in which we live. "What will it be like?" we may ask.

What will it be like when the guy holding up a sign in the Walmart parking lot finds a bath and a home and self-respect? What will it be like when the man who came to our church because he's struggling to stay clean from the drugs he's been addicted to all his life, finds the church embracing him as one of their family? What will it be like when immigrants can come out of the shadows and not be exploited by American businesses working under the table and at the same time funding politicians who manipulate our fear of the foreigner? What will it be like when my friend of years ago, whose mother killed herself years before that, finally gets an answer—or at least part of answer—to her question, "Why?" What will it be like when I—and you—finally get it? Then, "The

LORD will reign forever / your God, O Zion, from generation to generation."

## A Prayer

God, we are grateful that you care about those we struggle to care about: the poor, the uneducated, the mindlessly conservative, the mindlessly progressive, the ones whose sexuality does not fit our ideas, and on and on. We are glad that you love them so that we don't have to try so hard to. Or maybe this attitude offends you, and you remind us that we also fit in one of the boxes marked "unattractive" or "undesirable" or "unclassifiable." Then we rejoice that classification interests you less than mercy, that identity matters less than grace. Help us to trust that fact and so to trust you. Amen.

# 8

## All Used Up

*YHWH's word came to [Elijah], "Get up, go to Zarephath, which is in the territory of Sidon, and stay there. I have instructed a widow woman there to take care of you." So he got up and went to Zarephath. While he was standing in the city gate area, there was a widow woman there gathering firewood. He said to her, "Please give me a bit of water from a pot, and I will drink." So she got him some. Then he said to her, "Please give me a few bites of food you might have on hand." She said to him, "As YHWH your God lives, I don't have as much as a biscuit. All I've got is a handful of semolina and a little oil in a flask. So I'm gathering a couple of sticks of firewood so I can go and make it for myself and my son. We will eat it and then die." So Elijah said to her, "Don't worry. Go, do as you plan, but also first make me a little bit of bread out of it and bring it to me. Then afterwards make some for yourself and your son. For thus says YHWH, Israel's God, 'A pitcher of semolina will never run out nor the flask of oil run dry until the day when YHWH sends rain on the earth.'" So she went and did as Elijah instructed. She and her household ate for days. The pitcher of semolina did not run out nor the flask of oil run dry just as YHWH promised Elijah.* (1 Kings 17:8–16)

Sometimes waking up in the morning is not that easy. Sometimes because you didn't sleep enough. Sometimes because your pillow was a stone, and your dreams no different than the horrors of lying awake. Most of all, it is difficult to get up in the morning when you have reached a decision about the future and realize that you have none; your decision is irrevocable, final. So it is in our story. It must have been difficult waking up that morning for the young woman whose name we've lost, the widow of Zarephath. Perhaps she looked over at her little boy, all that was left to remind her of a dead husband. There was almost nothing to feed him. Today they would begin to die.

How had it come to this? The drought played its part, of course. Some said the drought was deity's way of warning the powerful to pay attention. If so, it was not entirely successful. The rich were doing just fine, thank you. For the poor, it was a different story. No one could share, there was nothing to spare. Empty breadbaskets and empty bellies except for a few.

Perhaps she remembered the hushed conversations with those who had more. "Isn't this your mother's jewelry? Are you sure you want to part with it? Oh, I wish I could give you more, but business is hard up these days." It's hard to forget your neighbors' "no I can't help you," and hard to keep saying to an eager but increasingly thin boy who loves his mother, "Oh no, son, I'm not hungry. You eat," when even the smallest child could see fear in her eyes and discern that odd odor of the malnourished. Today we eat, and someday soon we die. What could be clearer? Waking up to that plan is a difficult proposition.

So there she is, our anonymous widow, gathering sticks enough to cook a last meal. Did she feel the pitying eyes of neighbors? Or, perhaps not pity really, but rather a sort of grim relief. Pity would imply a willingness to help, but relief comes when we know that the other person's very existence no longer challenges us to offer a cup of water. For, when the poor die, at least the rest of us have the satisfaction of lament and guilt, the voyeur's ultimate pleasure.

When your plans are made and you have accepted your fate, meeting a stranger who promises to bring another one presents difficulties, especially when the stranger is one of those wild-eyed prophets coming from the desert, the sort who has seen things no one else had—God, perhaps. The trouble with those who see God is that sometimes those so bedazzled cannot see anything else for the glare. Or sometimes they see everything as it is, not as it seems to be. Which way the prophet will go—that's anybody's guess.

So it is in our story. God says, "I have commanded a widow woman there to support you." It's not clear that God had bothered to tell her yet, but the plan is in place. The prophet will speak and, against every impulse in the human soul, which tends inevitably to self-preservation and the blindness we amusingly call common sense, she agrees to prepare the last meal not for her hungry son, but for the strange man from the desert. She who has nothing to give becomes the giver, and in doing so, she whom her neighbors have abandoned and left for dead—this is what pagans do; it's what makes them pagans—becomes the hostess, not just for a prophet used to the service of less communicative waiters who can only croak "nevermore." Hospitality is the foundation of all society. To refuse to accept from another is the ultimate violation of human trust. Conversely, by placing himself in a position of dependence, the man who spoke to God could allow someone else the chance to live fully.

It's such a simple story, this one. It's a story of divine provision, of never-failing Wonder Bread and extra virgin olive oil. A woman who had resigned herself to death reenters the world, not just as a recipient of someone else's generosity, but as a conduit of grace to others. A prophet—and all of us readers—learns to look beyond his usual circle of contacts to find God at work.

True, the story presents all sorts of conundrums: Why did the God who could set up a raven airlift let a stream run dry? Why send a prophet to be fed, not at home, not even by wealthy Gentiles who might welcome him as an interesting diversion at their cocktail parties, but by the poorest of the poor, and a woman at that? Why? But in addition to all our questions, the answer sounds forth. This is a story about God's hospitality to the smallest of us.

More than that it is a memorial to a prophet who stood up to power and embodied in his life a radical obedience to God, and to an otherwise forgotten woman who had given up hope. Thus, it memorializes the human race as a whole, since most of our species are poor, obscure, and struggling. The story reminds us that our task of Christian service and leadership around the world cannot be tamed and domesticated in the channels we often seek to make them run in. But there is a deeper sense in which the real hero of this story is a God whose care extends to pagans, to the frightened, to the despairing. This God offers hope by placing those who have met him face to face among those who have not. (And, by the way, it's not always easy to tell who is who.) God takes us from the valley of despair and the cesspool of guilt to the mountain of hope, where we can enter the heavenly banqueting hall and share in a bounty that knows no limits.

In our pagan world, in a world of swelling GDPs and ever more capable armies, of growing poverty and declining life expectancies in the poorest parts of the world, the people of God easily begin to practice an accounting system quite alien to God's. We give the microphone to the shrill voices telling us that all is well, all is well. We strut and fret our hour on the stage, hoping that our words are more than sound and fury, and that they do signify something. Which they do not. And in our use of noise to silence the vulnerable, we forget that God—whose opinion, after all, may be the only one that counts—follows a different accounting system that provokes strange words like, "I have commanded a widow to care for you," or "I am the resurrection and the life," or even, "Death will be swallowed up in victory." Now that's something to get up in the morning for!

## A Prayer

O God of the poor and the prophets, why tell us such strange stories of one person at death's door relying so closely on another? Why not tell us hero tales, for we wish to be David or Achilles or Patton on his mighty tanks. Why not remind us of our infinite potential and so encourage us to do good? Doubtless, you know best, and it may be that you are onto us and our pretentious, narcissistic ways. If that is so, then we must admit that our plans look a lot like the widow's: today we will eat, and then we will die. We don't know what to do with jugs that never run out of flour or oil, though your abundance has reached us so that we worry very little about food. We worry about being taken seriously and other such luxuries. Help us. Amen.

# 9

## Teaching Theology
## in an Increasingly Religious Age

*YHWH has given me*
  *the tongue of the learned,*
*to know, to aid the weary,*
  *to arouse a word.*
*Each morning, YHWH rouses up my ear*
  *to listen like the learned.*
*YHWH opens my ear,*
  *so I am not embittered,*
  *nor turned about.*
*I gave my back to the smiters,*
  *my cheek to the strikers.*
*I did not hide my face*
  *from abuse and spitting.*
*But YHWH helped me.*
  *So I was not disgraced.*
*Therefore, I stiffened my resolve [literally, made my face*
  *like flint],*
  *and so I know that I shall not face shame.*
*My defender is near.*
  *Who will quarrel with me? Let's stand together!*

46

*Who is in charge of my defense?*
    *Let him approach me.*
*YHWH helps me.*
    *Who will mistreat me?*
*All of them are like folded clothes*
    *that a moth eats.*
*Whoever among you honors the* LORD
    *should hear God's servant's voice.*
*That is the one who goes in dark places—*
    *no light for him!*
*This one trusts in* YHWH's *name*
    *and finds repose in God.*
*All of you fire-kindlers,*
    *spark-lighters*[1]
*walk in your firelight,*
    *among the sparks you've kindled.*
*From my hand this will be yours—*
    *you will dwell in a place of pain.* (Isaiah 50:4–11)

Teaching. Learning. As women and men pursuing those purposes, it is fitting that we hear the words of James and Isaiah, bracing as they are. For me, our text raises the problem of the teacher—the source of knowledge, the content of instruction, the structure of learning, yes all this, but more importantly questions of character and purpose. "The LORD gives me the tongue of the learned." "Do not be many teachers." "Watch your tongue, which is both creative and destructive." "Remember that great teachers face fierce opposition." All of these sober warnings and scoldings and challenges remind us that the teacher answers a noble summons to surprising joys that follow from the embrace of a purpose higher than ourselves.

In recent years, I have had many occasions to think about the art of teaching as a species of the art of living. You see, in 2014–15

---

1. The text here is obscure, but this translation makes good sense of the Hebrew consonants as they have been preserved.

I spent four and a half months doing research in East Jerusalem, Palestine/Israel, and another four and a half in Seoul, Korea, teaching at several seminaries in three distinct theological traditions. Along the way, I experimented with living as a Christian in environs outside my customary haunts, where I was a member of a minority in some way or another—of skin or tongue or faith or all three at once. To be a teacher when you don't know the language properly, to learn alongside others when no one is obviously in charge—well, you see the task.

Still, today I don't feel like talking about challenges and threats, warnings and admonitions. In our regimented world, and our regimented church, we strive ardently enough to maintain the status quo that we know deep down is unsustainable. We know all about challenge. Enough of all that! Let us speak today not of the brown and gray drab soul of the over-privileged West searching frantically for some experience that might mean something, anything at all. Let us not speak of that. Nor of the thousand idle issues that roil our churches and leech away our time as "responsible" leaders. No, let us look beyond them to something else. As William Butler Yeats says in his "Dialogue of Self and Soul,"

> When such as I cast out remorse
> So great a sweetness flows into the breast
> We must laugh and we must sing,
> We are blest by everything,
> Everything we look upon is blest.[2]

Today, let us join our text, the ancient prophecy of weal and woe, in the quest for the majestic freedom of looking upon all things as blest. Our age, especially outside the West, is a time of religion's increasing influence.

As I say, the text from Isaiah 50 comes from that part of the book most closely associated with the return from Babylonian captivity and most deeply implicated in the poet's search for beauty and purpose in the dazzling green and red and blue of the renewed

---

2. William Butler Yeats, *The Collected Poems of W. B. Yeats* (Ware, UK: Wordsworth Poetry Library, 1994), 200.

world of living things and lively people, speaks of one who learns and teaches in the school of suffering and of hope. (And, yes, they are the same school.) This prophet reveals the teacher as one who listens, who suffers, who speaks out and speaks up. Consider these things.

First, we teachers hear of the transformation of the prophet's ear, of God's opening it so as to make discernment possible. This was already an old image in the book of Isaiah, going back to the original prophet's call in chapter 6 to speak biting, clear words of rectitude to a mob of unwilling listeners. These men and women, generations of them, focused so intently on the comfortable patterns of their lives that they could not yet imagine anything else even when calamities befell neighbors just down the street. They would not—and because they would not, they could not—hear. Divine words of doom and of hope fell upon closed ears and closed minds. And so the later prophet, heir to the tradition of courage, counts himself blessed that, in God's grace, he at least can hear.

Now, hearing others well is not easy in our distracted world. We move, all of us, from one transient sensory experience to the next, unable to still our hearts long enough to perceive anything in its true nature. We cannot, with Yeats, cast out remorse or feel the blessing flow into our chest because we are too devoted to conforming to the culture of melodrama masquerading as reality to be free enough to hear and see and smell and taste and touch the world around us or within us as it truly is. Our ears may remain waxed over without our realizing it, the muffling of the cries and the songs, the sobs and laughter of the world seeming to be normal from long usage. And so the prophet bids us teachers hear.

And also, in the second place, the prophet welcomes teachers to the world of suffering, not indeed for its own sake, but as an inevitable by-product of the announcement of hope. This may seem a strange thing to say. And yet the suffering that the prophet faces in Second Isaiah, culminating in his being buried with the wicked rich and despised and rejected in the famous chapter 53, comes not from doomsaying like Poe's raven—nevermore. No, the most strident opposition, then and now, faces the prophet of true hope. For true hope originates from the awareness of the profound tension built into the world between what God intended to create and what has come to be. Remember what Lewis Carroll puts in the mouth of Tweedledee: "Contrariwise, if it was so, it might be; and it if were so, it would be; but as it isn't, it ain't. That's logic."[3] Sometimes the things that "ain't" are the ones that ought to be. And the audacity of hope prompts opposition, precisely because it calls into question the things that are true and good and right, or at least inevitable. "If anyone suffers as a Christian," says St. Peter. If anyone suffers for hope . . .

Yet suffering alone cannot bring about learning or produce the ideal teacher. The prophet's last move in our text speaks of the teacher's trust in the providential care of the Almighty. We hear of faith. This is the third thing.

Yet to hear of faith, a teacher must listen most carefully, minutely to her or his surroundings. The blustering, pompous, self-promoting speeches of weird-haired politicians or plutocratic televangelists or plasticized media darlings do not reveal faith, at least not in God. For that, we must listen to the silences of life. We must seek the vacant spaces where broken men and women hide, or rather where those who acknowledge the universal human reality of brokenness seek refuge. Out of the silence comes truth, and only the still voice can speak clearly enough for the closed-up ear to hear. For there alone is a small human being courageous enough to trust solely, fully, completely, perceptively in God. Since atheism is the most potent opiate of the people, clear-headedness captures those who can see in unjust suffering the soul's road to God.

Today, as I hear this text from the book of Isaiah and reflect on my role as a teacher of Scripture, a high calling and a weighty burden, I find freedom on this road, for we do not travel it alone. Over the past year, I have learned about more of my fellow travelers catching sustenance in God's truck stops. I walk with Dev, who aspires to return to Bangladesh to build schools and churches. And Mun Pan who pastors in the refugee camps of Myanmar. And

3. From *Through the Looking Glass*, chapter 4, in Lewis Carroll, *Alice in Wonderland and Through the Looking Glass* (London: Penguin, 1998), 157.

many other men and women in whose hearts burned a hope for a different world because their ears hear a gentle promise.

Let us not be many teachers. But since some of us are, let us press on with full confidence that the One who is our refuge has not welcomed us alone, but all who toil and sweat and bleed and weep, the abused and spat-upon. They are our fellow travelers, and we are learning their song and sharing their laughs, and so are blessed. May you discover that, as I have.

## A Prayer

Most merciful God, you have brought us to this new day with its wonders and challenges. When we are afraid, you do not desert us. When we are too proud, you challenge us so that we do not hurt ourselves and others. When we are lonely, you surround us with clouds of witnesses. Be among us today as we work to help your church grow in its calling to bear your easy burden for the sake of the whole world. Through Jesus Christ, our Lord, who reigns with you and the Holy Spirit as one God, now and always, we pray. Amen.

# 10

---

# Releasing All Restraints

*Isn't this the fast I choose:*
*    releasing wicked restraints, untying the ropes of a yoke,*
*    setting free the mistreated,*
*    and breaking every yoke?*
*Isn't it sharing your bread with the hungry*
*    and bringing the homeless poor into your house,*
*    covering the naked when you see them,*
*    and not hiding from your own family?*
*Then your light will break out like the dawn,*
*    and you will be healed quickly.*
*Your own righteousness will walk before you,*
*    and the LORD's glory will be your rear guard.*
*Then you will call, and the LORD will answer;*
*    you will cry for help, and God will say, "I'm here."*
*If you remove the yoke from among you,*
*    the finger-pointing, the wicked speech;*
*if you open your heart to the hungry,*
*    and provide abundantly for those who are afflicted,*
*your light will shine in the darkness,*
*    and your gloom will be like noon.*

*The LORD will guide you continually*
*and provide for you, even in parched places.*
*He will rescue your bones.*
*You will be like a watered garden,*
*like a spring of water that won't run dry.*
*They will rebuild ancient ruins on your account;*
*the foundations of generations past you will restore.*
*You will be called Mender of Broken Walls,*
*restorer of Livable Streets.* (Isaiah 58:6–12)

## Words at a University Graduation

I am grateful to stand here today with men and women who are not only friends, but partners in an extraordinary mission, the pursuit of the betterment of humankind. We are gathered here today to celebrate the work you have done and to consecrate the work you will do to aid everyone you meet in their pursuit of justice for all and peace for all in our world.

Yet in a truer sense, nothing we say here today can do justice to the occasion or add to the significance of the events that brought it about. Your sacrifices, your commitments, your free and dissident acts of joy are their own celebration. We come together today only to add to the party a little—and to wear these funny gowns, which are designed for just such occasions.

So today I will borrow from the prophet who gave us the words of Isaiah 58. The prophet spoke to men and women who also, like us, were trying to build a better world. They had experienced the terrible trials of war, the cruelties of deportation and exile, the horror of having nowhere to call home. But they had survived, as humans always find a way of doing. They had done more too. They had gone home. And in both places, beside the slowly moving canal waters of Babylonia where they hung their harps and the fast-flowing streams of Palestine, they had sung the songs of Zion. And they had found God.

Yet their dreams, like all of ours, had a way of drifting off, for in waking we find that the world has not stopped to honor our dreams, but its relentless toil had continued. The world still ran its merry race to—where exactly? Life without the dreams of a better world leaves the soul dry and dead, captive to the forces of tyrannical political systems and unrestrained markets—pick your flawed system carefully, please. So here we find the prophet inviting the people of Israel to a destiny that is always tied together with the destiny of others. Loosen every yoke. Loosen every yoke.

The essence of Christianity is the liberation of the human heart from the shackles that strangle it and slow its beating down until death mercifully comes. Christianity involves the pursuit of human freedom—freedom from oppression of many forms, freedom from the ever-present need to succeed and impress, freedom from the tyrannies of fear and envy that make it possible for the hungry and the full, the orphaned and the over-protected to live side by side, but not together. This is the yoke from which we are to be freed.

Now we must admit that not everyone sees Christianity this way. For some, it is a conspirator in the plot to keep humans chained or as Karl Marx famously put, both at once "the cry of the oppressed creature" and the "opiate of the people." And to be sure, some Christians have lent support to this not unkind but still terribly limited view of faith. Today the church, of all places on earth, must be a refuge for all who would be free of the yokes that weigh us down.

What we need, then, is the one thing that allows us as Christians to go forth and to achieve. That thing is hope. Not wishful thinking or fond desires, but the confidence that despite all appearances to the contrary, good will win in the end, and sooner rather than later. We gather together as people of hope, firm in the conviction that the last word has not been written about the human race. We are here today because we are sure that, though our world presents us enough defeats, enough tragedies, we do not tread life's path empty-handed. The toils ahead of us will not overbear us because we hope in the One who makes all things new.

Hope is that most elusive of virtues. True, it does not quite rise to the majestic heights of love, the cardinal Christian commitment that can cast out fear and allow us to imitate God. Hope comes a close second, and yet it is often misunderstood, corrupted into its poor cousin optimism or good cheer, Babbittized[1] in order to mask complacency and smugness, those mortal enemies of faith in God. Yet hope is the great experiment that is Christianity.

In our own time, the Christian thinker whose work is most associated with hope is the German Reformed theologian Jürgen Moltmann. Let me commend to you his autobiography, *A Broad Place*.[2] There he talks about his experiences as a nineteen- and twenty-year-old prisoner of war at the end of World War II, during which he had been drafted into the Wehrmacht while still a teenager. Sometime at the camp, a chaplain came and brought the men Bibles. "Some of us would certainly rather have had a few cigarettes," he says. But in the course of reading the Bible he encountered the gospel of Mark and near its end the plaintive cry of Jesus, "My God, my God, why have you forsaken me?" Moltmann writes about that discovery, "I felt growing within me the conviction: this is someone who understands you completely; who is with you in your cry to God and has felt the same forsakenness you are living in now. I began to understand the assailed, forsaken Christ because I knew that he understood me."[3] He understood me.

Christian ministers acquire many skills. They can read Greek and talk about the church fathers and mothers and preach and counsel. Maybe they want to do those things better, but they have made a good start. Yet the most important thing any minister carries about is this discovery that Brother Moltmann also made in the burial ground of false hopes, the prison camp. "I knew that he understood me." Christian hope depends on the conviction that

---

1. This made-up word is based on Sinclair Lewis's character George F. Babbitt (from his book *Babbitt* [New York: Harcourt, Brace, 1922]), who is a sort of model of smugness and complacency.

2. Jürgen Moltmann, *A Broad Place: An Autobiography*, trans. Margaret Kohl (Minneapolis: Fortress, 2008).

3. Ibid., 30.

God, the creative sovereign of everything, understands the human soul and seeks to help it long purely for the things that matter. With us, God longs for justice among human beings and healing in the creation. With us, God longs for the end of wars and the forgiveness of wrongs. With us, God longs for all things to be made new. And, while our longings can often be frustrated, the desires of God become realities in due time, so that God's promises are sure.

From that basic realization that God understands us, we can offer two further ideas. First, hope involves more than a mental attitude inside an individual human brain. It is rather about the practices of a community—the Church—as it longs for, and works for, the healing of the world. Basic Christian practices such as baptism, the Lord's Supper, intercessory and contemplative prayer, fasting, confession, healing, and the sharing of goods all express the abiding confidence that the bounty of God suffices in the face of all shortages, that forgiveness can heal all wounds, and that human relationships can be built on honesty and acceptance rather than hierarchies rooted in fear and subordination. These practices feed hope in the individual soul, or at least they can if we do not surrender them to the very hierarchies and power structures they most naturally wear away.

Second, hope offers us a powerful lens through which to gaze at the world. It allows us to see accurately, to distinguish between the real and the fake, to identify obstacles to human flourishing. It helps us put a stop to cynicism, often masked as realism, which dogs our paths. Hope provides a way to examine social structures in light of the sin they embody and the new life they might bring. No system that denies opportunities for human redemption can long stand, and no such system deserves the support of Christian men and women.

Now, claiming to be for hope might seem like steadfastly supporting motherhood or being adamant for apple pie. It sounds like a cliché, a throw-away line. But in truth, many people in our world wonder if we Christians are for it. We seem to them too ready to condone state violence, to side with power rather than virtue in political or economic structures, to abandon the good news of the crucified one who understands us for the tranquilizing moralisms of religiosity. So advocating hope is not so conventional a thing after all. It requires some courage in the face of a secular world that has assumed too readily that humans live alone on earth and bear responsibility for its fate without reference to a God, and thus without any prospect of a transcendent reality. Christians refuse to accept our era's "whatever" attitude, the thin tolerance that in our time has replaced the Christian commitment to love. We ought not abandon the pursuit of being better than we presently are—marks us as different kinds of people. People of hope will seem out of place in our world obsessed with celebrities and money-grubbing.

So today, go forth in hope. Heal the sick, comfort the afflicted, afflict the comfortable. Be men and women of courage and of good cheer. Resolve to make a difference. And surround yourselves with those who wish to do likewise, for those of us who serve a living and active God, the merciful and gracious liberator of slaves, the One who vindicated the righteous by raising Jesus from the dead as the firstfruits of those who sleep, do not go forth to battle in futility with insuperable foes. We go forth, rather, to a cruciform life that finds in every tragedy the seeds of hope, in every defeat the resources for victory, and in every sorrow the distant echo of joy. You are going forth to such a life. Congratulations!

## A Prayer

O God, today we are hungry and thirsty, not just for righteousness (because that's a big commitment) but for the courage to hunger and thirst for you. We are overstuffed with ourselves, full of our pride and our achievements and our petty vanity. We desperately crave approval from others even when we know there can never be enough. Today we are hungry for some of the wrong things because we struggle to name the real things we lack.

O God, today we are hungry and thirsty. Be our food and drink. And let us banquet with all the rest who are hungry and thirsty too. Amen.

# 11

---

# Education in Suffering

*Then God saw their [the Assyrians'] deeds, their repentance of their evil ways, and then God relented from the calamity that he had announced for them and did not do it.*

*But Jonah was horrified and extremely angry. So he prayed to Y*HWH*, "Y*HWH*, isn't this what I expected when I was on my own soil. This is the very reason I decided to flee to Tarshish. For I knew that you were gracious and merciful, slow to get angry and abounding in love, relenting from disaster. So now, Y*HWH*, please take my life from me because it's better for me to die than to live." But Y*HWH *said, "Is it good for you to be this angry?"*

*Thereupon Jonah left the city and set up shop just to the east of the city, making for himself a rude shelter so he could sit in its shade while he watched what would happen in the city. Y*HWH *God, meanwhile, instructed a gourd plant to grow over Jonah to provide shade for his head, to rescue him from his own calamity. Jonah was overjoyed about the gourd plant.*

*However, at sunrise the next day, God instructed a worm to infest the gourd so that it withered. As the sun beat down, God instructed the dry east wind, so the sun*

*struck Jonah's head so that he almost passed out. Then he*
*asked to die and said, "My death is preferable to my life."*
*Finally, God said to Jonah, "Is it good for you to be*
*angry about the gourd?" And Jonah said, "It's good for me*
*to be angry enough to die." So YHWH said, "You worried*
*about the gourd, which you didn't labor over or make grow.*
*It sprouted one night and died the next day. Shouldn't I*
*worry about Nineveh the great city, which has a popula-*
*tion of 120,000 people who don't know the difference be-*
*tween their right and their left, besides many animals?"*
(Jonah 3:10—4:11)

Every speaker goes through several stages after accepting an invitation to speak. The first stage is *rejoicing* because you get a chance
to be with good folks and share your ideas with them. The second
stage is *remorse* when you realize that, normally, all things being
equal, you should say something when you're the speaker. That
doesn't always happen, but it is the expectation. The third stage is
*resolve*, when you decide to persevere, out of shame if nothing else.
And the fourth stage is *resignation* when you say what you wish to
say in hopes that it will mean something.

Jonah the reluctant prophet experienced the four Rs, though
not in the right order and with much less pleasantness than one
could have wished. Little children know his story, the story of a
prophet swallowed by a sea monster. This is not the story of Elijah or Elisha the miracle workers or of Amos or Micah the great
excoriators of injustice or of Isaiah with his visions of peace in the
world (swords into plowshares and all that!). Jonah's is a story of
radical failure amid great success, of reluctance to communicate a
message of doom because it might lead to a change of life and thus
a renewal of hope.

The book of Jonah has long intrigued readers, partly for the
whale story and partly because his whole attitude reeks of self-im-
portance and a radical distrust of the audience he was supposed to
address. How could he object to God's willingness to save penitent
sinners? How could he not take pride in being the most successful
speaker in human history? After all, his one-sentence speech led
to the repentance of an entire empire, from the monarch down to

the donkeys and oxen (who doubtless had less to be sorry for than the people did). And yet the little parable about the cantankerous prophet ends with a series of questions, the most haunting one from God: "Should I not be concerned?"

As an educator, I like questions. And in particular I like the question God and Jonah are discussing, which is, how do you understand human suffering and God's response to it?

There are some lessons to be learned here because one of the most important things Christians and other well-meaning people do is reflect on human suffering. In universities like mine, we train doctors and social workers and psychologists to help remove it. We train theologians, historians, and philosophers to help us understand it. We educate musicians and artists to help tell about it faithfully. Each of us deals every day with men, women, and children who suffer in myriad ways. We Christians in particular have our own special angles on suffering because we serve a God who experienced it in the person of Jesus Christ and who betokened its ultimate demise by raising the same sufferer from the dead. We are certainly not escapists, nor do we offer glib, but ultimately demeaning answers.

Before passing to answers, then, we need to feel the full force of God's question of Jonah, for its answer is not at all obvious. After all, the Ninevites were not people who simply misunderstood things but were basically well-meaning. Not at all. Nineveh was the capital of the Assyrian Empire, which like all empires to one degree or another rooted itself in the creation and distribution of human suffering. For readers of the Bible, "Assyria" and "Nineveh" conjured up images of devastation, traumatized refugees, burned out towns, dead bodies. Destroying Nineveh would not have been a gratuitous act of divine power but a matter of simple justice and a way of preventing further tragedy. Jonah calculated all this and feared that God's math might not be quite so secure as his own. A merciful God might not take seriously enough human suffering because that God might just lump the persecutor and the persecuted into the same category. So this is why Jonah ran. He could think of no other answer.

If we can understand that, we can understand the power of the book's final question and even why it might end with a question at all. (After all, most biblical books end with a greater sense of resolution than that!) So the question, "Should I not be concerned?"

It's unobjectionable (unless you're Ayn Rand or some other sociopath) that it's good to care about people. We are in the business of bringing justice through giving care. Jonah wondered if YHWH cared enough about Israel to protect it, and YHWH argued that his care extended even wider than Israel. But what does care for others look like?

The medical anthropologist Arthur Kleinman, in a beautiful article in *Harvard Magazine* a few years ago, reflected on his experiences as the caregiver for his wife, Joan, formerly a leading scholar of Chinese classics and now a sufferer with Alzheimer's. In contrast to the psychotherapeutic assumptions dominating American culture, in which such a disease can only be a burden, he argues that one's response to such an undesired situation determines what sort of a person one can be.

> Caregiving is a foundational component of moral experience. By this I mean that we envision caregiving as an existential quality of what it is to be a human being. We give care as part of the flow of everyday lived values and emotions that make up moral experience. Here collective values and social emotions are as influential as individual ones. Within these local moral worlds—family, network, institution, community—caregiving is one of those things that really matters, but usually not the only thing.[1]

What has this to do with justice, whether ours or God's? A great deal, in fact.

For most human beings, the task of justice happens not only in the public arena, but much more frequently in the mundane rhythms of life with a spouse or children or parents or coworkers.

---

1. Arthur Kleinman, "Forum: On Caregiving," *Harvard Magazine* (July–August 2010), 27.

Any theology that relegates such features of life to the margins will inevitably be trivial (no matter how soaring its rhetoric) and unsustainable. Anybody who locates justice chiefly in the realm of politics, and therapy or healing chiefly in the realm of family, perpetuates the kinds of splits that have created modern culture's profound dislocation from itself.

What if we reversed the assignments? What if we thought of justice as part of every particular part of my dealings with others over a long time? Justice between strangers can never take the place of justice among friends.

"Should I not care?" Jonah had to learn the lesson that care could happen on the largest and smallest scale, at a single moment and over a period of centuries. It comes from an attitude toward life. Jonah's God becomes the model of that attitude. The question is, will we?

## A Prayer

O God, the truth is that we wish to manage your distribution of mercy, to calculate the best odds of improving the human condition (as if there were just one). Help us to embrace the freedom of your graciousness. Amen.

# 12

# Caring Enough

*[Jesus] came to Nazareth, where he was raised, and went
into the synagogue on the Sabbath as usual. When he
got up to read, they handed him the scroll of the prophet
Isaiah. He unrolled the scroll to the place where he found
what was written:*

> *The Lord's spirit is on me,*
> *Having anointed me to tell the poor good news,*
> *Sent me to preach parole to the prisoners,*
> *Sight to the blind, deliverance to the oppressed,*
> *To preach the year of the LORD's approval.*

*Then he rolled up the scroll, handed it to the atten-
dant, and sat down. Everyone in the synagogue was star-
ing at him.*

*He began to say to them, "Today this scripture is ful-
filled in your presence." Everyone paid attention, amazed
at the gracious words come from his mouth. "Isn't this
Joseph's son?" He said to them, "You might say to me this
parable, 'physician, heal yourself. Do in your hometown
what we heard you did in Capernaum.'" Then he added,
"Truly, I tell you there were many widows in Israel in the
days of Elijah, when the sky was closed for three years and
six months, since there was a major famine in the land.
Yet Elijah wasn't sent to anyone except to Sarepta of the*

*Sidonians to a widow woman. Moreover, there were many lepers in Israel during the time of Elisha the prophet, but none of them was healed except Naaman the Syrian.*

*Everyone in the synagogue was infuriated at hearing these things. They stood up, rushed him out of town, and took him to the bluff of the hill on which their town sat in order to push him off. But he got away.* (Luke 4:16–30)

Homecomings are hard under the best of circumstances. You have already discovered how it is. You've returned home at Christmastime after a semester, and your parents have painted your room and rented it out to someone else. All the posters of baseball players on your walls, you know, the ones signed by Josh Hamilton or Pedro Martinez or Satchel Paige, all got thrown out, and now your little sister's Hello Kitty things decorate the walls. Homecomings are hard. And they get harder, I am sorry to tell you, though they eventually get sweeter too for most of us.

It's curious to me that the early Christians remembered a story of homecoming associated with Jesus. This one appears in all four of the gospels in one form or another, a very unusual phenomenon, since few other stories do. Jesus comes to his hometown, Nazareth, and on the Sabbath he shows up in synagogue. When the time comes to read from the Bible, the presider asks him to read, and he unrolls the scroll of Isaiah to what we could call chapter 61: "The Spirit of the LORD is upon me, and he has anointed me to bear good news to the poor; he has sent me to proclaim liberty to captives and seeing to the blind; he has sent me to offer release to captives and to proclaim the year of the LORD's favor." What a great sermon! What a great homecoming.

Except that it wasn't. As the sermon progressed, Jesus made what seemed to be a horrible mistake. He told the truth. He pointed out that not everyone wants others to have liberty and sight and so on, and that not everyone will receive it. In fact, those most confident of it may not receive it. And so his audience, people who remembered him as a child, who saw him grow into a man, turned on him and tried to kill him. The homecoming had gone awry.

But as I think about this famous story, I wonder a couple of things. First, what does it take to make others want to kill you? What about the message of Jesus is so controversial? Part of the answer is that no one tries to kill another over platitudes or truisms. Jesus' offer of peace and healing seems to have an edge that beauty pageant speeches don't. Partly this is because Jesus wants his followers to do something about this dream and not just talk about it or hope that somehow it might happen someday. Jesus wants us to live it. He wants us to serve the people in prison, to offer some real good news to real poor people, to care about the fate of our fellow human beings. And he wants us to do these things in the simple trust that God cares about these issues more than we do.

And that leads me to the second thing I wonder about. If you believe, as Christians do, that God takes an interest in the affairs of human beings, you have to wonder what God's priorities are. All of us must make decisions about what to care about. I, for example, do not care if the NFL players and owners, the millionaires and billionaires, reach an agreement on how to divide up the loot they've taken from us. I don't care about a lot of things that flow across the news. I do care about the fate of the Middle East, persecution of minority groups in Myanmar, and the projects for drilling wells in Sub-Saharan Africa. And I do care about the kind of education my students get, wherever they're from. I want it to be deep and real and challenging and not just a ticket to more money and prestige. You care about that too.

But what does God care about, or better yet, whom does God care about? I think we are comfortable with the notion that God cares about *us*. We have a history. We stand on the shoulders of faithful people who went before us. We received the Spirit in baptism. And here we are to worship, bow down, and say that you're my God. So of course God cares about US. But what about others?

Does the welcome extend to, I don't know, the guys in jail for robbing a 7–Eleven or the people on the streets hawking papers on Sunday mornings or the people who clean your university dormitories for a much lower salary than students' parents make? And does that care imply any need to change on our parts, perhaps even a surrender of our privileges or a questioning of our confidence? Or maybe it means for some of us a greater trust in God and a liberation from our own guilt at not doing enough? It depends on who you are.

Who you are, Luke's little story reminds us, depends in turn on what you care about. Jesus invites his disciples to be care about one thing, or as Søren Kierkegaard reminded us, to be pure in heart. This does not mean that we all give up all earthly pursuits and move into some sort of monastic community. Some people need to do that, but not most of us. It doesn't mean that we have ignored all social rules. Weirdness is not, strictly speaking, a requirement of Christian faithfulness. But it does mean that we get to do the things we do with the biggest possible set of reasons. We can solve calculus problems or split atoms or learn tax law or analyze Beowulf or whatever else we do to the glory of God, knowing that all of it—all of it—can contribute to the ongoing work of making all things new. We don't have to do great things, but we can do all things with love. And in living lives of simple trust in the Almighty, we can see ourselves as we truly are, people in deep need of God's freely offered gift of sight and liberty and acceptance. Nobody here is entitled to it. But all of us can receive it, even those we wish could not.

## A Prayer

Lord of all the nations, hear our prayer as you hear the prayers of all who seek you and speak to you in every language. We call you Gott, Hananim, Elohim, and a thousand other names because you have called us by name to be in relationship with you. Together we pour out to you our deepest hopes, our most terrifying fears, our likes and dislikes because we trust you to shape these things into the image of your son Jesus Christ.

We thank you, O Lord, that Jesus commanded those who came before us to go into all the world and make disciples so that the gospel should come to us through them. We thank you for knitting us all together so that we might share our food and water with the needy, visit those in prison, clothe the naked, and in more and more parts of our lives imitate your generosity to us. Amen.

# 13

## The Families of God

*Seeing the crowds, Jesus went up the mountain and sat down with his disciples gathered around him. Opening his mouth, he taught them this way:*

*Blessed are the poor in spirit, for theirs is the Kingdom of Heaven.*

*Blessed are those weeping, for they shall be comforted.*

*Blessed are the self-restrained, for they will inherit the earth.*

*Blessed are those hungering and thirsting for righteousness, for they will be satisfied.*

*Blessed are the merciful, for they will be shown mercy.*

*Blessed are the pure in heart, for they will see God.*

*Blessed are the peacemakers, for they will be called children of God.*

*Blessed are those persecuted for righteousness, for theirs is the Kingdom of Heaven.*

*Blessed are you whenever they insult and persecute and slander you (falsely, for my name's sake). Rejoice and celebrate, because your reward is great in Heaven. For this is how they treated the prophets before you.*
(Matthew 5:1–12)

Recently, my wife spent a semester in Korea, communicating with our adult children mostly online. In May, we Skyped with them, we also remembered that in Korea May is a month for celebrating another set of blessings, the gift of family. Children's Day, Parent's Day, Couples' Day, Adults' Day, and Teacher's Day—all of these come in May as we celebrate the work of many people who make sure that there will be a next generation of human beings and that they will inherit a better world than we did. Although all of us struggle in our families in one way or another, and none of us has a "perfect" family, there can be a beauty in family. There is a beauty in the smiles of children, in the sacrifice of adults, and in their sharing together. There is a beauty in gray hairs, and there is a beauty in small voices of those just learning to walk and talk. All this beauty is worth celebrating.

But there is a greater beauty underlying all these things. There are blessings within these blessings. For as Christians we believe that God has called all of us into a family, consisting of many families, but also bigger than any of them. And this family can care even for those who otherwise are without parents or children or spouses, because this family has a merciful parent in God. By this family, of course, I mean the group of disciples whom Jesus called to follow him, the church.

As we think about Christian families, we must also confront a bigger question. And that is, what does it mean to be a Christian? It will be difficult for me to ask what it means to be a Christian father raising Christian children to serve in Christian ways until I find some answer to that prior question: what does it mean to be a Christian?

There is probably no better place to go for an answer to this question than Jesus' Beatitudes in the Sermon on the Mount. Despite their familiarity, however, these beautiful lines also have a troubling aspect because Jesus clearly has an understanding of "blessing" that differs from how many of his followers understand it. Some people understand blessing in almost purely material terms: a new house, a nice car, a good job, admission to a prestigious university, and so on. However, this materialistic point of view reduces God to a sort of investment counselor in the sky, a being who can give us what we always wanted. But this is a sorry sort of God and not the one the Bible proclaims or Jesus reveals.

Jesus' understanding of blessing, to the contrary, takes seriously the fact of suffering in the world. He embraced and sanctified this suffering by experiencing it himself. And so in his life he endured poverty and ridicule and rejection. And then he died the most violent and disgraceful death possible. He never enjoyed prosperity or even a happy family life, unless we think of his disciples as his family, for they did truly love him, and he loved them. No, the Jesus we read about in the Gospels was not very blessed by the materialistic standards we modern Christians sometimes apply.

So what does he mean by blessing? Two things are worth considering. One is that when he uses the word "blessed," he is not the first person to do that. Already in the Old Testament, quite a few texts speak of the blessings that people can receive from God. For example, Ps 1 speaks of those who are blessed because they do not "walk in the counsel of the ungodly or stand in the road with sinners or sit in the seat of the mockers" but rather "delight in the Lord's law and meditate on that law day and night." In other words, these people have made a moral commitment to be part of the solution rather than part of the problem, and they are passionate about learning more and more how to love God and love their neighbor. Or take Psalm 119—the longest chapter in the Bible by far—which opens its 176 verses by speaking of the blessings of those who are "walking in the Lord's Torah" and then says in verse 2, "blessed are those keeping his testimonies, seeking him with all their heart." These people are blessed because they passionately pursue a relationship with God. As St. Augustine said, their soul is restless until it rests in God.

But the thing is this: the blessing they receive is not different from the pursuit. They do not do a job in order to get a spiritual paycheck at the end. They certainly do not perform some sort of good deed so they can bribe God into giving them material things. Rather, they realize that the pursuit of a relationship to God *is* the ultimate blessing. The life of the Christian is its own reward. They know what Jesus will later say in the Sermon on the Mount: "seek God's Kingdom, and all these things will be added to you."

It follows then that the Beatitudes speak to people who have already thought a lot about God's blessings. Moreover, in the Beatitudes, Jesus blesses those who are suffering: the poor, the sad, the meek, the ones strongly desiring justice. He also blesses those who try to serve the suffering, who empathize with them: the merciful, the peacemakers. Most of all, he blesses the ones who are persecuted because they try to do good in the name of Jesus Christ. These are the martyrs and saints on whose blood the church is built. These are the people who endure hardship for the sake of the Gospel. These are the members of our family not just of the past, but in many parts of the world today.

Now Jesus does not simply leave the suffering people of the world with the vague feeling that God somehow loves them even when it does not feel like it. No, he says that these people will receive what they need. The poor in spirit—or in Luke's version, simply the poor—receive not the wealth in this world, things that perish and do not bring true happiness. They receive the Kingdom of Heaven itself. And the same is true, by the way, of the persecuted. God's dawning Kingdom has as its chief citizens the very people who live at the bottom of the current age. And this is not all. The mourners receive comfort, those who refuse to take advantage of others and use their power for their own gain inherit the earth, and the pure in heart—there aren't many of those people, are there?—get to see God. God reverses the fortunes of the world and refuses to take its decisions about our lives as the final verdict. The gross injustices of the world do not stand in the end. Evil does not triumph over good, nor pain and suffering over health. In the end, all things work as they should, and as God originally intended them.

But for now . . . For now, we remain in a world in which we must hunger and thirst for righteousness. We desire to see a world of justice and peace—righteousness—precisely because we do not yet see it here. We have some idea of what it would look like if it came, but it is clearly not here yet. And yet we are convinced that the God who raised Jesus from the dead, who didn't just let him linger in the tomb forever, is also at work to bring about the transformation of all the human race. And this is why we hunger and thirst for such a reality. We can almost taste the day when there is no war, no broken families, no abused children or mistreated elderly parents, no neglected soul. We long for such a reality, and we commit our lives toward living as though it were already here. We want to be citizens of the Kingdom of Heaven as God is bringing it about. We seek righteousness with all our hearts because God is seeking this same thing for us. All of these things make us what we need to be.

So, you may ask, what does this have to do with families? And how does it relate to this family of families that makes up a church? The answer is, a lot. The Beatitudes of Jesus reveal those attitudes he finds most important. They also invite others to take up their place in the work of God in the world. These words are at one level a call to action, and in another way they remind us that we do not act alone but rather hand in hand with God.

So what should we learn from them? First, I note the call to action. Already, most of us work day and night to do the things we do because we believe that this is the right thing to do. But occasionally we must step back from our work and ask ourselves whether what we are doing is the right thing. Sometimes it is not.

I know that as the father of two young adults, there are things I could have done better when they were children. I should have spent less time at my job and more time working for their spiritual welfare. Even now, I can do a better job of maintaining my own spiritual health so that I have something to give to my family and to other families. The greatest gift we can give each other is spiritual maturity, a life of integrity manifested in love for God and love for neighbor. Everything else is simply a bonus.

So, yes, the Beatitudes are a call to action. They call upon us as Christians to ask what we can do to serve. And they call upon us to dream of a new world.

But there is something even more vital here. The Beatitudes also make an announcement. They declare that God is doing something in the world, and this something is for the benefit of humankind. The Beatitudes say that God looks at the world of people and sees that some people hunger and thirst for justice or weep or mourn or make peace. And since God wants human beings to have enough of the things we truly need, God responds to human need. No, that's not quite the right way to say this. Rather, our cries for justice, our weeping, our attempts to make peace, our desire to be pure in heart—all these things come as a response to God's desires. God's work is primary, and ours follows it.

In the Beatitudes, Jesus announces that all of this is true, that the Kingdom of God is coming. Since it is in the nature of announcements that those who hear them must respond, whether positively or negatively, Jesus' announcement is also an invitation to our response. And so the question before us today is, how do we respond to God's announcement? Christian families and Christian individuals are those who believe that God is working in their lives in the ways that the Beatitudes set forth.

And so let us be of good cheer. Let us be steadfast and resolute. And let us all—fathers and mothers and brothers and sisters and friends in whatever condition we find ourselves—let us all resolve that together we shall be a family, one of the many families who make up the mighty family of a gracious God. For then our gracious Father may receive us with welcoming arms and a smiling face. "Well done, my beloved children."

## A Prayer

O God, it seems that the righteous do not ask for beatitude. Nor do we, though our righteousness is suspect. Rather, we pound on your door asking for peace and fullness and justice and spirits ferocious against evil but gentle toward others. We are grateful for the bonds of biology and experience and values that link us together. We humbly thank you for them, for they are often their own beatitude, and they point us to the intimacy that we hope to enjoy with you. Amen.

# 14

## The God Who Frees Us from Evil

*When Jesus went to the region of the Gadarenes, there met him two demon-possessed people who habitually emerged violently from the tombs such that no one could walk that road safely. They cried out, "What do you want with us, son of God? Have you come to exorcise us before the time?" Now, at some distance there was a herd of swine feeding. So the demons begged him, "If you expel us, send us into the herd of swine." He said to them, "Go out." And as they left, they entered the swine, whereupon the whole herd stampeded down the slope to the Sea [of Galilee] and died in the waters. The swineherds fled, entered the city, and told everything that had happened with the demon-possessed people. So the entire city went out to meet Jesus, and upon meeting him, they encouraged him to leave their environs. Embarking in a boat, he departed and went to his own city.* (Matthew 8:28—9:1)

Today is something different. Yesterday they were mad, really. Today their minds are clear. Yesterday they lived alone under bondage to forces far beyond their control, not of their own making. Today they live at home, breathing free. Yesterday their history was lost, their future gloomy. Today they live with simple human hopes for families and meaningful work. Yesterday, the Gadarene demoniacs lived with one foot in hell, and with the other they blocked the road for all who sought to live gently ordinary human lives. Today, well, today is different.

Matthew's story of an exorcism is duly famous for its terseness, its depiction of a hit-and-run raid by Jesus on the strongholds of darkness—Gentile country polluted by swine, and populated by understandably terrified people who ask him to leave. Parts of the story seem difficult to follow: Why did Jesus go there? Why did the demons object to being exorcised? Did their statement, "you have come here before the time" indicate their outrage that he had cheated by conquering evil before the resurrection, or is it simpler, just the natural protest of beings who did not court death for themselves even when they brought a living death to others? And what does Matthew mean by radically trimming his Markan source, moving the site of the exorcism twenty miles closer to the lake, and removing many explanatory clauses in the story, if that is indeed what happened? Perhaps most of all, what are we "enlightened" moderns, with our convictions that evil originates mostly from individual human choices and can thus be remedied by reeducation, to make of such a story? Perhaps it confronts our superstitions, just as we accuse it of offering its own.

This story signals something important about Christian experience. It insists that Jesus Christ brings healing to all under the yoke of evil—the Jesus whom early Christians remembered did not merely teach insightful words or cheer his disciples with an arm on the shoulder or an occasional post-fishing-ordeal beachside breakfast. His ministry used power for healing the sick, stilling the waters, raising the dead, and, in short, confronting powerful forces of evil, whether embodied in a puppet king or a Roman procurator or, more dramatically, doubly incarnated in a demon inhabiting poor human beings. The Jesus who shows up in the gospel did not lead disciples to a purely introspective religion that imagined that telling the story of faith was the same as living it. No, Jesus figures here as God's answer to cosmic evil, the messiah of Israel who bears in himself the past and the future, the treasured memories and fond hopes of not just God's people, but all the world.

And yet, what do we make of such a story? The trouble with tales of exorcism is not merely that they strain the credulity of modern people with a scientific bent. After all, we can allegorize away the epistemological scandal if we want to. The larger trouble is that we often are not sure if we believe in the existence of evil in a strong sense. Part of our uncertainty arises because of the very success of Christian language and practice in vanquishing the snakes from every emerald isle. Evil, we have concluded, has been defeated, and so we need not give it power by believing in it.

I wish that were the full explanation, but in truth it does not seem to be. Rather, the problem with believing in radical evil in the way the early Christians did is that such a view calls into question our human pretensions, our sense of autonomy and lifelong purposefulness, and our conviction that somehow, in some way, we can conquer all, if not through love then through knowledge or creative leadership. The early Christians assumed that the chaos of the world led inexorably to evil on a gigantic scale that only a sovereign God could end.

The German New Testament scholar Ernst Käsemann put it this way in a 1987 lecture recently translated, "Possession denotes . . . what in the history of dogma is called 'original sin,' that is an addiction to earthly powers and forces . . . The creature is always only under one lord and in the service of his kingdom."[1] An addiction to earthly powers and forces.

Sometimes that takes the drastic form that requires the old-fashioned ministry of exorcism. Of that we may be sure. But mostly it takes subtler and far more dangerous forms, dangerous because they do not seem to be addictions at all: the addictions to military domination, to economic exploitation, to racial superiority, to intellectual security. They even mask themselves in the once beautiful but now somewhat frayed clothes of morality and religiosity.

Käsemann, one of the truly great scholars of the past century, knew whereof he spoke. His daughter Elisabeth was one of the

1. Ernst Käsemann, *On Being a Disciple of the Crucified Nazarene*, trans. Roy Harrisville (Grand Rapids: Eerdmans, 2010), 204.

disappeared ones during the Argentine dictatorship of the 1970s. Murdered—or maybe we can say martyred—for her solidarity with the poor in opposition to a brutal regime and its fellow travelers, she was commemorated by George Harrison in his semantically fractured song "Dear One." The addiction to power and even a false sort of order brings about the destruction of the world. Love of power prevents us from telling the truth.

Hence our story. Jesus' defeat of the evil powers is a key element of the Christian message and a key presupposition of the Christian life. We are all freed demoniacs. Our soul whispers too, yesterday in longing for the coming of the Lord to our broken world. And today in thanksgiving for the one who has freed us too and who will not leave our strange, strange land but will abide here with us until all is made new. Today is a new beginning. Today, well today is something different.

## A Prayer

O God, we are not crazy or threatening or driven to desperation. Our caves seems comfortable enough, and we welcome travelers who pass by them, as long as they do not linger too long or demand too much. The demons that haunt us have grown fat and a little lazy under our influence. Believe us when we say so.

O God, perhaps we are a little crazy, just a little threatening, a bit despairing. We ignore evil, calling it freedom. We accept oppression as the condition natural to "those people," a necessary stage in our ever-bettering prosperity. We think that nothing much awaits us beyond the grave, that ours is the best possible world. Our madness has grown comfortable, well-worn, familiar.

O God, we have no herds of pigs to receive our demons. Please drown them in some other way so we can be lucid again. Amen.

# 15

## The Judas Memoirs, or Thoughts of a Lost Brother

*When Judas, the one who betrayed him, saw that Jesus had been condemned, he was remorseful and returned the thirty silver coins to the chief priests and elders. He said, "I have sinned by handing over an innocent person for execution." But they said, "What do we care? You fix it." So he hurled the thirty silver coins into the temple and withdrew. He went out and hanged himself.* (Matthew 27:3–5)

### What Would Judas Say for Himself?

You should have been there. It was an amazing day, First Day was. (What do the goyim call it? Oh yes, Sunday.) There we were walking into the city, and not your average Passover party either. Yeshua of Nazareth, our rabbi, riding a donkey. The crowds gathered around us and shouted all kinds of things. "Here is Jesus of Nazareth, king of the Jews. Let us praise the Almighty." Palm branches on the ground and people peering out of windows, and I especially loved watching the soldiers nervously shuffling at the street corners and watching the crowds. But we were disciplined,

disciplined. No stone-throwing yet. No riots. We remembered what the rabbi had taught us.

It has been an interesting week since then. We've walked in and out of Jerusalem, back and forth across the Kidron to the Mount of Olives. I have to tell you that I love this time of year with the almond trees and olive trees blooming and the grape vines sprouting. Blessed be the Almighty who brings forth fruit from the ground. We have walked in and out of the temple, and our prophet spoke of how not one stone would sit atop another soon enough, and then would come the end, the triumph over evil, the full blooming of the covenant. Peace. Peace. And then we will sit under our own vine and fig tree and no one will make us afraid. Nobody.

It's hard to think right now, with all this movement. But I can remember many things about the rabbi. He has been our teacher. Blessed are those who hunger and thirst for justice, he said. Blessed are the poor, for they will see God. We no longer have to be afraid. The sons of light will defeat the sons of darkness. That's why there are twelve of us around him all the time, each symbolizing a tribe, each symbolizing the victory of light over darkness in the last day. I can't wait, I tell you that.

He's a great teacher. I love to see him out-argue those Pharisees. He makes it look so easy. A parable is all it takes. Let's see, what was it? Oh yes. There was a woman who had only two coins. Poor woman! Two coins that she lost and then went to a lot of trouble to find again. And that's what the Kingdom is going to be like. We lost it through our own disobedience, as the prophets said. But now we will get it back because we seek it diligently, and God is good.

The rabbi always reminds us of how good God is, and how powerful. This is why he does miracles. I will tell you about them. My friend Peter's mother-in-law was sick, almost dead, poor woman. Jesus just touched her and healed her. She's still cooking for people. And then there was that little girl whose father (what's his name? Joram? Jairus?) asked for help and Jesus just said to the little child *talitha qumi*—reminded me of Elisha. And then there was that night when we had been talking about Jonah all day and he woke up and stilled the storm on the lake. And then there was the time when all those people were following him—he brings hope to the poor, you know—and nobody had brought any food for some reason, and he fed everybody with a lunch. I'm not sure anybody would believe that if they hadn't been there, but I was there. And of course in the New Era, this sort of thing may happen all the time, or maybe it won't because everyone will have enough to eat and, besides, Torah will be in their hearts.

So that's our rabbi. He is a powerful man. Now I know what you're thinking. You think power is just what the Romans have. After all, their soldiers are always hovering over us every time we go pray in the Temple. And we even walk through the galleries to the House of God because their puppet Herod built these places. The legions aren't that far away. *Pontius Pilatus praefectus Iudaeae.* Very tough, very bad man. But his time will come. All their time will come, and rabbi Jesus will be there to make it happen.

This is my confession. It's been quite a week, like no other I've ever had. Maybe no one has ever had one like this since our teacher Moses brought our ancestors from Egypt and took them to Sinai. *Lammah rageshu goyim? Ule'umim yehgu riq?* Why do the heathens rage and the peoples plot pointlessly? The Lord, blessed be he, will smash them in pieces! And our rabbi will be at the head of the line as the anointed one before he sits at God's right hand in glory!

And that is why I am confused on this fourth day. Passover is upon us. It is time to act. It is time for deliverance. A new exodus is possible. God's power can be shown to the world! And so today I do not understand. Today the rabbi took us all aside and he said—let me get the words right—"you know it's two days till Passover, and the son of man is going to be handed over to be crucified." The religious people are plotting against him—betrayed by his own people, but that's what happens to prophets, right? But not this time. Not this time.

The trouble with being powerless is that someone promises you power, and then you find out it's not really going to come your way. Is that happening? Or is the rabbi just having a bad day? Too many emotions in play? Too many emotions. I don't understand. It's not the first time. That's true. My friend Simon Petros has told me that before. Judas Iscariot, he says, you just don't get it. Maybe by the next First Day, it will all make sense.

## A Prayer

God, what a strong word betrayal is. That a small man could sell out the savior seems impossible, too grandiose for our kind. What drove him to it? Not mere greed or fear, surely, or perhaps the attempt to manage the future according to his own lights?

God, what a strong word betrayal is. Let it not apply to us. Amen.

# 16

## The Thief on the Cross

*One of the criminals hanged there spoke against him, say-*
*ing, "Aren't you the Christ? Save yourself and us." The other*
*rebuked him, "Don't you have respect for God since you are*
*also condemned? Yet we are justly punished, just getting*
*what we deserve. But he has done nothing out of place."*
*Then he said, "Jesus, remember me when you come into*
*your kingdom." And he said to him, "For sure, today you*
*will be with me in Paradise." (Luke 23:39–43)*

### Thoughts for New Theologians
### (Spoken in Zagreb, Croatia)

A few hundred meters from where I lived in the fall of 2014 in
Jerusalem, the Church of the Holy Sepulchre sits hidden among
houses and shops teeming with pilgrims, merchants, and a host of
other people. The church marks the traditional site of the crucifixion, burial, and resurrection of Jesus. And in truth, all the evidence
suggests that the real place must have been very close by and perhaps even where the tradition says. And so it is moving to see the
lines of men and women from every corner of the world, speaking
all its languages, coming to pray in a building parts of which

go back to the late Roman Empire, and other parts of which still exhibit crosses carved into the stone wall by the Crusaders. The Holy Sepulchre is the most holy Christian pilgrimage site on earth.

Today we are, if you will allow me to say so, embarking on a pilgrimage of sorts as well. Those of you who sit at the front of this auditorium in those wonderfully charming robes have earned a seat by your diligent work, your willingness to imagine new worlds, your sacrifices and your dreams. Congratulations to you. You are embarking today on a walk of faith as teachers of Scripture who will point others to the Crucified and Risen One and will help us all practice the life to which he called us, in which all of us beat our swords into plowshares and our spears into pruning hooks, in which the sick are healed and those pushed aside as "unworthy" or "weak" take up their rightful place as children of God. We need you because we need this vision.

So, before you go into the world as new theologians, let me remind you of one of the greatest of our number, a man whose name we no longer know, but who is also remembered at the Church of the Holy Sepulchre for very good reasons.

In our text from Luke, we read of a moment during the crucifixion of Jesus during which a man whose misspent life has landed him on a cross, a death fit only for terrorists and murderers and bandits, manages through his pain and humiliation to reach the very heart of everything you and I are studying and trying to live out. "Jesus, remember me when you come into your kingdom."

Luke, as so often in the Gospels, does not dwell long on this scene, allowing it to speak for itself across the centuries. We see something in this story that seems almost impossible. One man does what we would all do: grasp at the last desperate chance for a solution to our deepest problems while assuming that the answer will never come at all. The first thief I understand, because he lives all around us, and inside of us too. It's the second one who's the mystery. How did he see past his own physical agony, the burning and then numbness in his overstretched muscles, the rattle in his lungs as he lifted himself up to breathe, while pulling on the flesh that the nails had penetrated? How did he recall what he had heard all his life about the mercy of God to sinners who truly repent and God's concern for everyone, when his own life had betrayed all that was true and good and right? To be honest, I am not quite sure.

But the important point is that for one brief moment, the decisive moment, he understood everything clearly. He saw that the third man on a cross along with him and his colleague in crime was not who he seemed to be and that this apparent disaster that had befallen him—his unjust trial and execution—did not tell the final story of his life. No, the vision of the Kingdom that the third crucified man had spoken and lived for a while had a future because it spoke to the deepest longings of the human heart, and not just ours, but God's heart too.

Well, before we become too sentimental, perhaps we should look carefully at what our fellow thief says, "Jesus, remember me when you come into your kingdom." I am struck by the first word. He uses the third man's given name, not as a disciple would (they call him "master"), but as a close and intimate friend would. Or, in the Gospel of Luke, as people in trouble do, for in that Gospel the ones who address Jesus by his given name include demons possessing persons (4:34; 8:28), the ten lepers (17:13), and a blind person (18:38). No one else addresses him in this way. In other words, for Luke and his readers, Jesus' given name has become associated with healing and divine mercy, which is why, in Luke, those addressing him as "Jesus" usually add some other honorific title such as Lord or Son of David and then ask explicitly for mercy. This fact is very striking, because it means that Luke wants us to hear the thief's request as another example of healing and salvation. One helpless human cries to another by name and seeks relief from pain and all that goes with it.

And then there is the request itself: "remember." This verb immediately takes us back to the Psalms, which repeatedly ask God to remember people in distress so that they can be saved. And so we read things like, "Remember your mercies O LORD and your steadfast love that is from of old. Do not remember my youthful sins and my transgressions" (Psalm 25:6–7). Or, "Remember me,

O LORD, with the pleasure you take in your people; visit me with your salvation" (Psalm 106:4). Or the deep philosophical question, "What is the human being that you remember him?" (Psalm 8:5). By memory, of course, the Psalms do not mean the offhanded recollections that come to us unbidden, triggered by smells or sounds or sights that connect us to something past, but something unimportant or fleeting. No, the Psalms mean the kind of memory that one must cultivate and work to access, like memories of the faces of someone we love or the texture of their hair or the words we used to say to them and they to us. This is the deep kind of memory that comes out of a relationship of mutual trust and concern. As the French philosopher Paul Ricoeur puts it, "We have nothing better than memory to signify that something has taken place, has occurred, has happened before we declare it."[1] And this is what the thief asks for on the cross: "Jesus," he says, "think deeply about me and be in relationship to me because I trust you in spite of everything." At that moment, he was almost the only person on earth who did.

And then there is the third part of his request, "When you come into your kingdom." The Passion story says that others commented that day on Jesus' so-called kingdom: Pilate mocked him, or rather all his people, by calling him "king of the Jews," while various parts of the mob, including its leaders, cruelly derided his kingship. And surely they had a point, for no one bows to a crucified king. No one imagines for one second that such total powerlessness can help anyone or make any positive difference in the world. No one except God and our crazy, mixed-up thief. They still think that the Kingdom in which the poor are filled, the peacemakers see God, and the mourners are comforted, and all the rest can become a reality. Only they.

What, then, does this story say to us? Perhaps a few things. First, I cannot help but remember that a hundred years ago in this part of the world a young man in his early twenties named Gavrilo Princip killed a man almost exactly my age called Archduke Franz

---

1. Paul Ricoeur, *Memory, History, Forgetting*, trans. Kathleen Blamey and David Pellauer (Chicago: University of Chicago Press, 2004), 21.

Ferdinand. And in doing so, he gave powerful people an excuse to kill European civilization and unleash decades of brutality, what Aleksandr Solzhenitsyn has called the century of the concentration camp. We can never forget the strength of bad ideas and the abuse of power lest we all end up in a tragic way. So today, my hope is that you, in your youth and your newfound knowledge and growing wisdom, will be forces for goodness and truth and will hold up the torch of hope that can light up even the most desperate soul. Remember who you are, and more importantly remember the one you follow, the Crucified One. For he heard the dying gasp of a broken soul.

So this is the second thing I hope for from you. Let us all train our eyes and ears and minds to attend to the work of God among us. Can you not see it, hear it, taste it? When we forgive an enemy, when we feed a hungry person, when we see beauty where it was not visible before, do we not also see the work of God? Let me be straightforward here. There are many things about Christianity that I do not like much. Sometimes we Christians are arrogant or indifferent or afraid. We defer to the rich and powerful unnecessarily often. And sometimes we dress up our will to power, as Nietzsche would call it, in the gaudy costumes of faith, hope, and love. Sometimes I wonder if it makes sense to continue with the church's game at all. Maybe you wonder the same thing. But when I begin to think that way, I am called back to a more fundamental truth. Yes, Christians have many of the same failures as everyone else, and sometimes worse failures in part because we know how to pretend that we are not sinners. We have learned the tricks of that game. But then there is the Lord we serve. The Lord who, over the numbness in his muscles and the rattle in his lungs could muster the strength to say, "Today, you will be with me in Paradise. You. The thief. Because I remember you." Let us go forth to point not to ourselves, but to that one whose name still comes from the lips of helpless people, as we all ultimately are.

## A Prayer

We seek to find you within ourselves and among your people.
*Lord, hear our prayer.*
We seek to find you in the face of the prisoner and the bruised back of the persecuted.
*Lord, hear our prayer.*
We seek to find you in the stranger, angel or not.
*Lord, hear our prayer.*
We seek to find you in our families and in our commitment to them.
*Lord, hear our prayer.*
We seek to find you in the things that supply our needs, and in the trust that you will provide them.
*Lord, hear our prayer.*
We seek to find you, though you are not lost, nor far away, nor elusive, but are everywhere, for in you we live and move and have our being.

And so we ask you to help us, to drive away our fear, and to give us a disposition of faith in the company of our fellow human beings.
*Lord, hear our prayer, and help us to hear your answer in Jesus Christ, by whose authority we pray. Amen.*

# 17

## Blessed Are Those Who Do not See

*Thomas the Twin, one of the Twelve, was not with them when Jesus came. So the other disciples said to him, "We have seen the Lord." But he said to them, "Unless I see the nail marks in his hands and put my finger in the nail marks and then put my hand in the wound in his side, I will not trust." So a week later, his disciples were again inside, this time with Thomas. Jesus came in among them, though the doors were locked, and said, "Peace to you." Then he said to Thomas, "Stick your finger here and see my hands and extend your hand to touch my side. Do not be untrusting, but trusting." Thomas answered him, "My Lord and my God." Jesus said to him, "Have you trusted because you saw? Blessed are those who trust without seeing." (John 20:24–31)*

Dear old Thomas. You've got to love him. Afraid, skeptical, unstampede-able. The sort of person who says, "I'm not saying I won't believe it, but I won't take your word for it. Not calling you a liar or anything. Don't get me wrong. Just sayin'. But for something like this, I've got to have some evidence." And then a touch, a look, and the expostulation, "My Lord and my God." His is not just any confession, but the fullest one in all the Gospels, the one presupposing a different view of reality—of divine transcendence and presence, of the boundary between life and death, and of the possibilities for God's mighty work in the world. Doubt and faith intertwine here, not as foes wrestling for mastery but almost as lovers, each finding a place in the human soul. Dear old Thomas.

Like many of you, I like Thomas Didymus, the twin, because of his frankness, his common sense, and his desire not to believe baloney. His search for clarity, and the Gospel's honesty about his and others' doubt, are both refreshing in our age of bright lights in your eyes and smoke in your face. The story has the precious ring of truth. Thomas's story reminds us that the road from doubt to faith is not always very long because living in either place requires a proper respect for our own humanity. "I am a human being" often is synonymous with "I do not know."

But there is more than that here, for Jesus does not merely celebrate Thomas's honesty or his newfound, intense faith. Rather, he breaks the fourth wall of the text, looks at us readers and says, "You are blessed even though you have not seen as our friend Thomas did." You are blessed because you believe.

I wonder what this blessing means. Does it mean that, if we accept a statement as true, we will receive some sort of benefit from that? Probably not, since John's Gospel does not use "believe" to mean merely intellectual assent, but rather radical trust. And probably not, because "blessed" seems not to involve receiving a Santa's grab-bag of toys like life, liberty, and the happiness finally caught up to. In truth, John uses this word "blessed" (*makarios*) only on one other occasion, at the Last Supper—or maybe we should call it the First Supper. After washing their feet, Jesus instructs his apostles to serve each other in similar ways, noting that the servant is not better than the master, nor the one sent than the sender. To be sent, to be an apostle, is to carry forth the practice of service. "If you know these things, you are blessed if you do them." That's John 13:17.

Both there and here in John 20 we have knowledge about the followers' relationship to the Lord, and this knowledge translates into action, creating a state of blessing. The blessedness may involve a cross with all the accompanying mockery and abuse. It may demand that we confess not only "Jesus is Lord" but "this person is my neighbor." It may mean standing up to evil men and women who would crush the weak in order to make themselves or their lackeys feel strong. But it is the way of Jesus and the way of Easter—to do the will of the one sending us *is* the blessing.

Blessing, then, describes an aspect of the relationship between God and us. Maybe we could say that faith describes our condition and blessing describes God's side of things, now shared with us. In fact, even this is not quite right, because faith comes to us as a gift as well, a response to the overwhelming encounter with God. We do not merely will it. It finds us. So, when Jesus says to Thomas and to those of us who find ourselves in his story, "Blessed are those who do not see and yet believe," he says in effect, "Look, my friends. You were not there that Sunday in that upper room. You did not have to face the terror of a hyped-up mob or a no-nonsense Roman procurator. You got off easy. For now. But you also can trust the Risen Lord. You don't have to be imprisoned by fear. You can come clean about your doubts, and even if you don't solve every moral or theological problem with arithmetical certainty, you can live together in trust because the Lord who rose from the dead and who took the trouble to gather one last lost sheep, dear old Thomas, has taken the time to gather you too."

## A Prayer

O God, we doubt, sometimes for learned reasons that have more to do with self-awareness of our understanding's limits than with our perceptions of your capacities. Sometimes we doubt more out of sorrow because our hunger and thirst for righteousness helps us see the terrors of the world, the futility of our plans for a better tomorrow. And sometimes we doubt because we perceive the glory of your vision for humankind and fear to enter into that vision. Help us to have the courage to doubt for the right reasons. But when we imagine your triumph over death, help us to have the courage to believe. Amen.

# 18

# Breakfast, Lunch, and Dinner
## after Easter

*When they had finished breakfast, Jesus says to Simon Pe-*
*ter, "Simon son of John, do you love me more than these?"*
*He says to him, "Yes, Lord, you know that I am your*
*friend." He says to him, "Feed my lambs."*
*    He says to him a second time, "Simon son of John, do*
*you love me?" He says to him, "Yes, Lord, you know that I*
*am your friend." He says to him, "Tend my sheep."*
*    He says to him a third time, "Simon son of John, are*
*you my friend?" Now Peter was grieved that he said to*
*him the third time, "Are you my friend?" And he says to*
*him, "Lord, you know all things; you know that I am your*
*friend." Jesus says to him, "Feed my little sheep. Truly, I tell*
*you that when you were young, you dressed yourself and*
*went wherever you wanted. But when you get old, you will*
*stretch out your hands and somebody else will clothe you*
*and take you where you don't want to go." He said this to*
*signify by what sort of death he would glorify God. And*
*then he said to him, "Follow me." (John 21:15–19)*

It's that time of year. All your brilliant thoughts over a semester
are coming to their glorious fruition in ways that will dazzle and
astound even the crustiest and most cynical of your professors. Or
you will realize that the reason you've had an extra hour for lunch

on Tuesdays and Thursdays is that you have never attended one of
the classes in which you are enrolled, and you are tempted to ask,
"What can I do now?" knowing that the answer, alas, is nothing.
It's that time of year.

For Christians, the week after Easter is also one of those times
of year. The boiled eggs are all destroyed, the marshmallow chick-
ens have gone on sale at Walmart (though given their half-lives,
no one knows why), and life has returned to normal. But not quite
normal, of course, because Easter is a holiday that refuses to be
domesticated, for at its core lies a very powerful story. A Jewish
peasant was unjustly charged, illegally tried, and cruelly executed
by the empire of his day, with the collusion of some religious leaders (professors and pastors and such). Like millions before and
after him, he was the sacrifice society pays for temporary order
and concord. Tragedy. Tragedy.

And it would be a story of tragedy if it ended there, a story
that would merit no holiday or remembrance because of its sheer
commonplaceness. Yet the story did not end there. Rather, it took
a very surprising turn when, early Sunday morning, the God of
heaven and earth vindicated the righteous, raised Jesus of Nazareth
from the dead, and made him, as the first preachers put, "Lord and
Christ." Easter is over but it demands a response of either belief
and the radical life transformation that follows belief, or else rejection and the acceptance of our fate that goes with that. Indifference
is not an option.

It certainly was not an option in the post-Easter stories in
the gospels, the one in front of us most of all. Here Peter, who has
denied Jesus three times and heard the rooster mark each denial,
must now have Jesus ask him three times if denial is his final answer. Fortunately, it is not. Peter responds to the gently demanding
questions by an affirmation of friendship with the Risen Christ.

Now some of us have heard the sermon about this text that
reminds us that Jesus and Peter worked awhile before agreeing
on just which Greek verb to use. Some preachers make a big deal
out of the difference between *agapao* ("to love") and *phileo* ("to
be a friend to"). But in truth, the New Testament and many other

first-century texts use the words more or less interchangeably. Peter isn't trying to finesse the question, and Jesus doesn't soften it at the end. In fact, in their conversation, they fiddle with the vocabulary quite a bit, and so we get three different words for sheep and two for tend or feed. So even if it is Greek to you, it wasn't to them, and they weren't making quite the point some people say they were.

But what point were they making? Jesus seems to say to Peter that it is all well and good to be back with the disciples now that it is perfectly clear that he is on the right side of history. Resurrections are amazingly clarifying events! But the commitment also has consequences, and powerful ones. One consequence is the move to feed the sheep, to tend to the spiritual needs of others who will follow Jesus. In John, the disciples have already heard Jesus' contrast between himself as the Good Shepherd and the hireling shepherd who cuts and runs at the first sign of trouble. "Which are you?" Jesus implicitly asks. And then it gets tougher still, because Jesus tells him that if he really wants to be in on the disciple thing, he must be prepared to die as a martyr, to follow Jesus to a cross. And not a metaphorical or symbolic one either, but a real wooden one with splinters and nails and torn skin and blood and taunting crowds. When Jesus calls us, he bids us come and die, as Dietrich Bonhoeffer would put it in the 1940s. Being ready for that is the only way Peter—we'll leave others out of it for the moment—can tend the sheep and thereby glorify God.

This is what Peter does. This is what all the early Christians were ready to do. Following Jesus meant the certainty of social alienation and the possibility of violent death. But they also thought it meant life with God, both now and forever.

What should we say about such a story? There are many things, but the one that grabs me first is simply that it could happen at all. After all, Peter had failed miserably. His presentation of his final project had been such a bomb that people still talk about it twenty centuries later. His entire life up until now had a giant red "F" written across the top of it. He had not shown friendship to the one he brashly called "Lord." Yet here was that same Lord inviting him back into friendship, back into a profound commitment that could only mean a new world. The promise of martyrdom becomes, for Peter, a sign of overwhelming grace.

That sounds paradoxical, admittedly. Our own culture is so deeply narcissistic, and that narcissism has rubbed off on Christianity to such an extent that we can hardly conceive of such a post-Easter view. This is why we can turn crosses into housing decorations and can treat church as a consumer good, a place we measure by its entertainment value. We are living out our own denials and have become deaf to the crowing of the roosters warning us of tragedy. And thus we become unable to conceive of resurrection either. Some of us even believe that we need not die. But Peter, at this moment a few days after Easter had ended, hears the most beautiful invitation of all: "follow me." And in so hearing he may also hear Jesus' earlier words, "Do not let your heart be troubled. You believe in God. Believe also in me. In my father's palace are many rooms." And one of them is for you.

## A Prayer

O God, being Jesus' friend is hard, not just because a cross overshadows us, but because we must tolerate all his other friends, the quarrelsome and terrified and petty ones, and even more insufferably the peaceful and courageous and broad-minded ones.

O God, being Jesus' friend is hard, not just because a cross overshadows us, but because we don't know how to feed the lambs and even if we do, we find them biting our fingers in trying to get to the food.

O God, being Jesus' friend is hard, not just because a cross overshadows us, but because it lives inside us too. Please don't take that away from us. Being Jesus' friend is hard, but being ours must be harder still. So we will take what you offer and try not to bite your fingers along the way. Amen.

# 19

## Beautiful Feet

*But how can they call on the one in whom they have not believed? And how can they believe without hearing about that one? And how can they hear without a preacher? And how can they preach unless they are sent? As it is written, "How beautiful are the feet of those who herald good news?"* (Romans 10:14–15)

Who sent you here? I'm not sure of the first time I heard that question. It might have been the summer after my second year of college when I spent June and July trudging door to door on behalf of the city directory gathering information about who lived where and what business did dry cleaning or fixed flats or sold insurance. There was the one moment when I knocked on the door of what appeared to be a sweat factory for sewing clothes and the nice Hispanic lady at the door quickly ran to the big white guy who threatened me with the menacing "who sent you here?" Sometimes, it seems, "here" is a place whose inhabitants seek obscurity and namelessness.

Or maybe it was earlier in life when I went next door to borrow something for my grandmother who was canning I don't remember what. Who sent you here? Well, that's okay then. Sometimes the question is an invitation to make a connection that spans time and memory and invites reminders of pleasure and joy. Who sent you here?

Being sent is not a notion we like to entertain, to be sure. It seems too un-autonomous, too threatening to our independence of mind and agency, too hierarchical. Or maybe it just seems too dangerous because sending implies a commission, a purpose, a message, and—God help us!—a commitment to something beyond my immediate self-satisfaction. It implies accountability. It demands a vision of what is not yet apparent, but may become real. And so being sent seems an unsettling concept.

This is, of course, precisely why the Apostle Paul brings it up in our text in the tenth chapter of Romans. He has been expatiating on the mercies of God that overcome all the divisions of reality that we face and that make it possible for the news of the Cross and the resurrection, the announcement of God's victory over sin and death, to reach both Jews and Gentiles. He has said that God keeps the ancient promises, brings the age-old dreams to reality, overthrows the old Adam and elevates the new. And yes, this fact poses the perennial problem that the prophets also faced, namely that some of us who should accept the message do not, while those who seem most estranged from God, most bereft of hope, unaccountably embrace the news that they too can be saved. The stakes in Paul's bid for a hearing are the highest possible because he's playing with funds drawn from the accounts of a God at work in the world to make all things new.

Nor is this grand discussion something abstract and distant for the apostle. No, the one sent, the one called, the one preaching good news—well that's just a description of his entire life since the moment on the road to Damascus when he fell blinded to the ground and cried out in surprise and undoubtedly physical pain, "Who are you Lord?" The startling answer redirected his life and, in truth, the whole future course of human history, for you and I, Gentiles all, sit here because of Paul, in large measure. Or rather because God worked through Paul to spread a vision of good news that could embrace all, both the heirs to the ancient promises and those of us who were aliens from them.

So, who sent you here? You may be asking yourself that very question, and you will ask it again in the future as you continue your studies and as you seek to understand yourself not simply as the autonomous thinker whose existence is the only certain thing, not just as the possessor of a very advanced, if somewhat gloppy, mental processor called a brain, but as someone sent, an *apostolos*, on a mission to announce and celebrate and live out the good news. It will be helpful to remember that all this luxury of study, of which there can never really be enough, serves the greater purpose of helping us understand the ways in which God works among us in Jesus Christ and therefore who God is as a covenant-maker, willing to get down in the mud with us sinners, and therefore what we learn about ourselves by gazing upon Jesus the exemplary human, the Second Adam, the leader of Humanity 2.0.

In truth, however, I do not believe that the greatest challenges we face today on the theological front are purely intellectual. Rather, they are the temptations of a deeply pragmatic, bottom-line-oriented sort of culture that expects results fitted to the prejudices of the self-appointed assessors. The sham hope we face today is that we might get spectacularly different results while pursuing the same comfortable methods, clearly an impossible task and an unworthy one. Parts of our culture, the parts that worship celebrity and status and wealth, teach that the real world is something other than the world that the Good God is redeeming through the Gospel. But this so-called real world, which shapes us far more than we know, simply represents the illusions of the old Adam that Christ exposed and destroyed. It seduces us through conformity and fear, and it is the last thing we need right now.

What we need instead is something far more radical and daring. We need men and women who see themselves as heralds of good tidings to the most broken among us. We need men and women who will bring healing to an Ebola patient—yes that's a dramatic case in the news not so long ago—but more generally we also need men and women who will worry more about the concerns of the weakest of us and less about those of the most powerful of us. We need to be able to join those who, like our master, the impoverished man from Nazareth, have nowhere to lay their heads, no status except that of a human being before God, and no protection from the forces of evil, whether the mockery of the settled and secure or the violence of a cross. These are the truth-bearers of humanity, the vehicles of God's grace, the messengers of the new life that comes to those who acknowledge our broken-ness. We need men and women who see the vision, which Paul and the other apostles saw, of a risen Christ who seeks to welcome all—all—into his embrace so that he may give them to God as a revivified creation. As I look about today I see those people, men and women who will speak and live so that others may hear the good word, "You are my people, and I am your God."

As someone who has also been sent, along with you, to carry good news to both tucked-away and wide-open spaces, let me en-courage you to embark on this journey. The road may be rough, the mountains may be steep, the forests may be dark, but the path leads somewhere glorious. And along the way, we will find joy together, so that we may invite each other into our lives with the great question, "Who sent you here?" God. Of course.

## Halting Attempts at Prayer

Attempt 1: O God, sender and receiver, source of life and destiny of us all, we much prefer receiving to being received, sent to rather than sent. We admit that feet can be beautiful, but walking on mountaintops sounds too difficult. We are not confident that you will send us to the right places.

Attempt 2: O God, sender and receiver, source of life and destiny of us all, we embrace the glory of being sent to faraway places, to cultures purer than ours in their exoticness, just waiting for us to declare them the "other" whom we must save. We embrace the grandeur of being sent.

Attempt 3: O God, sender and receive, source of life and destiny of us all, we see that everyone is sent someplace by someone. Where do you want us to go? Who should we be when we get there? Help us go where you already are so that we may be who we are. Amen.

# 20

## Workers Together with God

*For we know that even should this earthly dwelling place of ours disintegrate, we have a habitation from God, an eternal house in the heavens, not constructed by hands. This is why we sigh for our home from heaven, longing to be properly clothed so we that we won't be naked anymore. For we are burdened down as we long for that dwelling place. We don't want to be unclothed, but clothed so that death might be consumed by life. But the one working on us for all this is God, who gives us the down payment of the Spirit.*

*Therefore, we are always confident, knowing that those homebound in the body are really away from home with the Lord. For we conduct ourselves on the basis of trust, not sight. Yet we are confident and quite comfortable with being away from the bodily home and homebound with the Lord. We think it's more honorable to be homebound than away from home, that is, to be pleasing to God. For all of us—everything we have done, whether good or ill in a bodily way—must be revealed before Christ's trial bench.*

*Knowing what it means to be in awe of the Lord, we persuade human beings by saying: "let's be revealed to God." I hope it will be revealed through your conscience. We do not commend ourselves to you anymore, but we are*

*giving you opportunities to rejoice about you so you may
have something better than those who boast in appearance
and not in the inward reality. For if we are crazy, it's for
God. If we are wise, it's for you. For Christ's love binds us,
causing us to discern that since one died for all, all have
died. And he died on behalf of all, so that the living no
longer live for themselves but the one who died and was
resurrected for them. So then we no longer know things in
fleshly ways. Even if we used to know things according to
Christ's flesh, we no longer know things this way. Whatever
is in Christ is a new creation. The old things have passed
on, and the new things have come. All things come from
the God who reconciles us to Godself through Christ and
gives us the service of reconciliation. This is just like how
God was in Christ reconciling the cosmos to Godself (and
not keeping track of their infractions) and offering us a
word of reconciliation.*

*Consequently, we are emissaries on Christ's behalf, as
if God were making the case through us. So we do urge on
Christ's behalf, be reconciled to God. God made the one
ignorant of sin into sin for us so that we might become
evidence for God's righteousness in him.*

*As co-workers, we encourage you not to receive God's
grace in an empty way. For Scripture says, "At the right
time, I heard you, and on a day for salvation, I helped you."
Truly, now is the right time. Truly, now is a day for salvation.* (2 Corinthians 5:1—6:2)

## To Prospective Clergy

In Scripture, two voices stand out from the rest for their deep reflection on the nature of ministry. These two leaders explored the
psychic hinterlands of service to God in ways that, arguably, no
one else has. One is the prophet Jeremiah, the other, the apostle
Paul. On this day of rejoicing, I do not have the courage to hear of
the prophet's pain in the face of tragedy, so we will stay with Paul.

And what thrilling words Paul brings us in the paragraphs
just before the words above. "We walk by faith, not by sight." "We

have the Spirit as a down payment." "The love of Christ urges us." "A new creation—the old has passed away, and the new has come." Good and evil, mortality and immortality, nakedness and splendid clothing. Exhilarating words they are, words of power that encourage us to believe in all the possibilities and see visions and dream dreams of ourselves soldiering heroically in God's army, marching on to Zion, taking up arms against a mighty foe and slaying the old dragons of fear and hate. "*Now* is the acceptable time, *now* is the day of salvation!"

And yet . . . And yet surely you have the nagging suspicion, as I do, that hearing Paul this way is not quite right. After all, if I must walk by faith it is because for now the sky is too dark to allow sight. Down payments imply that the full reckoning must wait. Reconciliation implies alienation, estrangement. Good and evil—well, evil still exists in the world and shows no sign of retreating into its last resting place. No wonder that Paul goes on just after our reading to speak of the "endurance, afflictions, hardships, calamities," and like distresses he has endured in his role as emissary from the throne of God to the throne of Rome. Human short-termed, means-oriented power and the pursuit of power, even when masked in pious language and approved-of deeds, stands in sharp contrast to the ways of Jesus Christ. Perhaps we would have been better off with Jeremiah after all!

But then again, if we pick up the thread of Paul's reflections, they seem to go something like this: the gospel of Jesus Christ is the very good news that God exercises immense power in order to heal the world, and, astonishingly, we may join God in this great work. *Now* really is the day of salvation if we understand, with Paul, God's seamless interweaving of the already and the not yet. We are clothed, and we will be clothed. We are saved, and we will be saved. This life connects in an unspeakably deep way to the life everlasting, and we do not trade in the too few years we have here in order to earn a better life somewhere, or somewhen else, for the eternal life has already begun, despite appearances to the contrary.

In other words, Paul invites the Corinthians—and us—to consider a truly radical proposition. Ministry that comes from a deep awareness of the truth of the gospel does not depend for its success on mere human measures, however well-considered and sincere. True, we must have our priorities straight so that we will not pray as did one of our remorseful predecessors a century ago:

> Lord, we were so busy studying deep theological questions, arguing about the validity of critical enquiries as to the dates of the books of the Bible, preaching and hearing eloquent discourses, comforting and edifying one another, that we had to leave the Christless masses alone.[1]

But eloquent discourses and even pure hearts are not enough, for both easily suffocate under the weight of the so-called pragmatism that is now choking the Western church, according to which we imagine that we act alone for God rather than seeing God as the primary actor in the drama of redemption. "We then as workers together with God . . ."

Now, to be honest, we always face the temptation to make ourselves the center of attention in ministry, often smudging over the blatantly anti-gospel act of self-promotion by calling it "being real" when all we're doing is playing to the charming, narcissistic, consumerist voyeurism so characteristic of modern American culture. Christian ministry cannot be about the Christian but about the God we serve. A strong dose of Pauline theocentrism would do us all some good.

But there is more here, for ministry is always bi-centered, an ellipse rather than a circle. Like the prophets, we live as mediators between God and human beings, living into the goals of each so as to reconcile the two parties to one another. "We have this ministry of reconciliation," Paul says. Here, our very lives become models of bringing together God with the Christless masses, of which we ourselves are prominent members.

To live this ministry calls for more than the large, and I hope still growing, storehouse of knowledge you have begun to fill. Knowing Scripture, tradition, biblical languages, and

---

1. From a prayer by Alexander McLaren in his preface to Rodney "Gipsy" Smith, *Gipsy Smith: His Life and Work* (New York: Revell, 1906), 10.

demonstrating strong self-awareness and even the ability to communicate effectively—these measurable attributes that we call student learning outcomes—are not enough. We must also have vision, not just because without vision the people perish, but because without a vision we ourselves perish, perhaps long before we cease walking around.

So what is this vision? In our world riven by war launched by states, most notably our own, and by smaller groups taking up causes they imagine to be noble enough to justify murder, in our world polluted by the bald justification of greed as an expression of freedom and stained by the indifference and corruption of self-promotion—in such a world, what must our vision be? Paul helps us here in two ways, though almost off-handedly, when he refers to the "fear of God" and "not accounting for their trespasses." Awe before God. Cosmically inaccurate accounting. These are key ingredients of the vision.

The "fear of God" does not equal the terror of the guilty before the righteous judge. It is not a response of shame or a hopeless measuring of our now lost chances for survival. No, Paul draws on the heritage of the Hebrew Bible as it contemplates the wonders of God. To have awe before God is to be moved and shaken and changed, as a sensitive person may be while hearing a Bach cantata or seeing the Sistine Chapel of Michelangelo. But for us, awe is more than these experiences because the God of the Bible does not work primarily in paints or marble but in flesh and blood and souls, and the artistry involves human lives refashioned so that giving cups of water to the thirsty and clothing the naked and visiting the prisoner become a matter of course. Awe before God comes because we see that colossal power unites together both great love and rigorous justice, because the aim of both is to find the best for all.

We join, says Paul, the ministry of the God who does not track our sins in the heavenly ledger, much less in the fleshly log books of our brains, but ensures that the word of condemnation and failure not be the final epitaph of the human race. We join a ministry of prayer and service, of hands and hearts and heads and feet, of action and godly inaction. We join together, arm in arm, with the men and women who have gone before, in anticipation of those who will come after us, and we sing the songs of the human heart seeking to know the God who made us, for that song is but an echo of the great symphony of heaven itself. The old is fading away, and the new has come.

## A Prayer

O God, we enjoy work that matters, that improves the world, that feeds our souls more than the work that simply fills our pocket-books or brings us praise from others. Our teamwork, work as a team over time, gives us satisfaction and reminds us that something about our lives can matter even after all have forgotten our names except you. Be our mate, our companion on the way, our partner in announcing good news. Or rather, let us be yours. Amen.

# 21

## Seeking a Lasting City

*By faith, Abraham obeyed when called to go to a place he was about to receive as an inheritance, and he left without knowing where he was going. By faith, he dwelt in a promised land like a stranger, residing in tents with Isaac and Jacob, who were similarly called to the same promise. For he sought a city with foundations whose architect and builder is God. By faith, Sarah, though infertile, received power to bear a child at the right time because she considered the one who promised to be faithful. So from one source, and these persons as good as dead, many were born, numerous as the stars of the sky or the uncountable grains of sand on the seashore.*

*These all died in a state of faith, that is, without receiving the promised things. They saw them from a distance and greeted them, acknowledging that they were strangers and aliens on the earth. This is because people saying such things make it clear that they are seeking an inheritance. If they had been thinking of the place from which they came, they would have had a chance to return. But they sought something better, that is, heavenly. And for this reason, God was not ashamed to be called their God, for he had prepared for them a city.* (Hebrews 11:8–16)

Babies, cities, wanderers, trust. This text comes at a critical moment in the letter and in the life of the church to which the author writes. In elegant, highly educated Greek the author of this sermonic letter encourages his people to remember who they are as followers of Jesus Christ and to draw inspiration from those men and women of faith who have preceded them. Remember, he says, Abel and Abraham, Moses and Gideon, saints and martyrs all. Remember all the famous men and women of old, as well as those whose names are known only to God. Remember most of all Jesus Christ. And in your remembering, draw courage from their example so that you can persevere. Draw courage when fierce persecution threatens to degrade you and make you doubt God's love. Draw courage when the ease and comfort offered by a life that accommodates the world sedates your spirit with the ordinary drugs of living. Either way, do not give up.

This is one side of the coin. Our text is about human bravery, the daring to pack your bags, get out of familiar territory, take terrible risks, shed everything that is familiar and comfortable. That is the sort of courage that inspires all of us, and which we may see even in each other. And when it is directed at the noblest purposes of which humans are capable, it may rightly be called faith.

But there is another side of the coin, and this is the one I wish to talk about now. For at the end of the day, the text we have heard and the story of faith itself do not merely come down to human courage. It is not just about us, even the bravest and most admirable of us. It is also, or rather first of all, the story of God, the one upon whose promises Sarah and Abraham and countless other saints have relied.

This text portrays God as the one who calls, builds, and promises. Here we see in bold colors and sweeping lines a picture of a gracious Lord who invites human beings to join a quest in search of meaning and purpose in life far transcending the momentary goals of survival, much less the all too commonplace seizing and holding on to power or wealth or fame or comfort. I will tell you about it.

First, the God who calls. Our author has read the much older text of Genesis, which recounts the migration of Abraham and Sarah and their family from the comforts of Ur to the wild west of Canaan. We see their mistakes and even sins, but in the passing of time, all of that is washed away, as it is for all of us. And now Hebrews tells us only of the valuable part of their lives, their response to God's gracious call. There was, of course, nothing wrong with living in Ur, nothing amiss in living a normal life of producing and reproducing and dying quietly at the end. This is what we all do, and what Sarah and Abraham also did in their new land. But if they had remained at home, comfortable in their normality, there would have been no story to report. You never hear on the evening news the sentence, "Most people stayed home and minded their own business." And you never hear in Scripture that God tells people to mind their own business and take life easy. Saints are not made that way.

No, they were called to something more, just as we are. But why does God call them? That is the question. The answer is clear, but not easy to accept. According to Genesis, God intended to create something in the human heart that would bear fruit in a community of people over a period of centuries. This great project bears the name of Abraham's grandson, Israel. And through the people of Israel all the peoples of the world would be blessed. This is, in other words, a God who invites people into very, very long-term projects that will lift generations yet unborn to the life of the Spirit.

And then there is the second splash of brilliant colors here, the face of the God who builds. It's an arresting image that Hebrews borrows from several sources. Yes, the Old Testament repeatedly speaks of Zion or Jerusalem as the city of God's concerted attention, including both grace and judgment as needed. Indeed, the idea of a great king building a city according to a divine blueprint is even older than that. But perhaps the most immediate source is the philosophical discussion of his own time, for a generation earlier another great commentator on the Old Testament, a Jew named Philo from Alexandria, had also spoken of God as the great planner of the whole universe as a well-organized urban space in which the human soul could thrive. Hebrews seems to like this image, mentioning it twice in this reading alone.

God, he says, builds a city fit for human beings willing to enter the life of faith. God does not jam together slums of ramshackle and filthy hovels, nor construct sterile, inhuman rows of brutalist concrete apartment blocks for storing human bodies in their isolation from one another. No, this city includes parks and sunlight and space for meeting with friends and hearing music and seeing dance. In this city, babies laugh and old people share their stories with appreciative audiences. This city feeds the human soul rather than sucking life from it. And this is because, of course, the city's chief citizen is God himself, who joins the laughter and dances along with us. And this was the city that Abraham and Sarah really sought through all their meanderings down the stony trails of Canaan.

It is interesting to me that Hebrews claims that Abraham and Sarah sought a city. Genesis, of course, never quite says that, for the Old Testament conception of a promised land is more rural, appealing to the idea of the Garden of Eden rather than a crowded urban space. But for Hebrews, the choice of the city as the aspiration of the faithful reminds us that we do not do this alone. Cities by their very nature contain crowds of people, lots of people—masses of men and women and little kids, each with a dream, each with a hope, each with the passions of love. And each with the potential for good and evil. Hebrews reminds its readers that the walk of faith is not always solitary. Even in our most lonely moments, we travel in the company of a host of others, God most of all.

And now the third quality of the God who called the patriarchs and matriarchs: this God made promises. Not just rules. Not just creedal statements. Not just theological constructs. Promises. And these promises were of the boldest and most adventuresome sort because they committed God to dealing with human beings in all our weakness, while also inviting us to commit ourselves to working with an end in mind even when we cannot see its fulfillment at the moment or perhaps even in our lifetimes. This feature of our preacher's picture needs our attention because we may easily think in much too small ways. Even when do not confuse our own interests with those of God, we too easily knuckle under to the pressures of small-minded people, especially those willing to exert any means, no matter how unscrupulous, for fulfilling their own goals. Certainly Abraham and Sarah also faced that temptation. Saints always do. But what distinguishes the saints from the also-rans is that people of faith rest in the hands of the God whose vision is far bigger than ours, whose dreams for us surpass our wildest imaginations, and whose willingness to promise is matched only by a capacity to fulfill. In this God, they put their trust.

Babies, cities, wanderers, trust. This text comes at a critical moment in the life of the modern church as well. For today we face critical questions of our responsibilities to each other and the promises we see God fulfilling in our neighbors and fellow Christians. Yet we may face the future with courage and hope because we also trust the God of Abraham and Sarah, who has invited us to search and promised that we will find.

## A Prayer

O God, you have loved adventurous people, slightly mad people, to tell the truth. Sarah and Abraham as they shuffled from the neonatal unit to the social security office. Moses and Zipporah as they planned to defy the mightiest ruler in the world. You know their names better than we do. But we are not those people. That's the rub. We want to control and manage and plan and chart the odds. Big data rules our lives, leaving big dreams to fend for themselves. We are not those people you want to spend time with, for we have renounced madness and with it, faith. Help us find the way back to laughing with angels and facing down Pharaohs and living into a different world. Amen.

# 22

## Coming to Mount Zion, or Why Vision Matters

> For *you have not come to a touchable mountain burning with fire, to darkness, gloom, and storm, trumpet blast and the sound of speaking of which the hearers begged not to hear another word because they could not bear what was commanded (i.e., "And if a beast touched the mountain, it was to be stoned"). In truth, it was so terrifying that even Moses said, "I am afraid and trembling."*
>
> *Rather, you have come to Mount Zion, to the city of the living God, the heavenly Jerusalem, and to myriads of angels in joyful gathering, to the assembly of the firstborn written about in heaven, to God the judge of all, and to the perfected spirits of the righteous and the mediator of a new covenant, Jesus, and a purifying blood that speaks better than Abel's.* (Hebrews 12:18–24)

### For Christian Professors (and Students to Overhear)

Not long ago, as I already mentioned, I had the privilege of being a visiting professor in Seoul, Korea. That city of twenty-five million people is a crossroads of the world, a place where high-tech and old tradition live side by side and where the future seems to present itself. It was exciting to live in places that invites students to think globally, to love their neighbor, and to pursue academic and personal excellence. That is a vision worth pursuing.

And speaking of vision, today, let us hear this text from the epistle to the Hebrews, part of the book's climax. In this extraordinary text, the author of this letter invites his hearers, both ancient and modern, to look beyond the mundane experiences of everyday life and to imagine something that they cannot see or hear or touch. He asks them not to focus upon their own tasks, much less upon the petty ambitions that so often occupy all of our time. Instead, he wants them to consider the largest possible vision of humankind, the vision of men and women standing in the presence of God, not as fearful beggars hoping for a crumb or two from the master's table, but as beloved children eager to be in the presence of their loving father.

"Look," our author says, "we have access to something even better than the most extraordinary event that has ever occurred for human beings, the revelation of Torah at Sinai. That was the moment when ex-slaves knew—or should have known—that they were to be free. Free from the human tendencies to lust and steal and kill. Free from the desire always to beat the other person, to find advantage, to gain power. Free from the pursuit of false gods and false lords. Yes, Sinai was a marvelous moment, but we have access to something even greater. For we may come to God without fear because of the one who has gone there before, the pioneer of faith, Jesus Christ."

In saying all of this, the author of Hebrews invites those of us engaged in the noble profession of Christian higher education also to consider our own vision. We also must ask whether we are discouraged by the crush of everyday suffering or distracted by the flash and noise of everyday success or merely bored by the repetitiveness of everyday work. Have we lost the ability to see that everyday life is not all there is, and that in fact, we are called to something much more? This is the question that this text confronts us with.

What does such a vision look like? Of course, there can be many variations. Our musicians must help us hear beauty in its many forms. And our social workers must teach us what a well-functioning society looks like. And our business colleagues must help us imagine how to make people's lives better and protect our fragile world. And our theologians must help us understand the church's long encounter with God and the many ways in which we have talked about that and lived it out. So we all have important work to do.

And yet there are common elements of this vision, too, simply because though we are many, God is one. Our writer mentions several things that are worth paying attention to.

The first is that the vision is social. It involves not just individuals hoping to be saved, but entire groups, and even the human race as a whole. So here we read of Israel and the perfect saints and even the angels as what St. Augustine, in his great work the *City of God* called "a large part of this city, and indeed the more blessed part, since they have never been expelled."[1] That is, the preacher to the Hebrews has in mind a vision that embraces the largest possible number of intelligent, spiritual beings. His vision is the very opposite of small-minded or parochial understandings of the world.

This idea is extremely important because it reminds us that the Christian understanding of the world is not bound by the many ways humans find to divide ourselves from each other. We human beings have developed the uncanny ability to turn things that should be beautiful expressions of God's intentions for humanity—language and culture and even the life of the church itself—into ugly sources of division and conflict.

However, the ultimate vision of Zion, the vision about which our text speaks, does not allow us to continue in that way. There will be no divisions in heaven, no barriers erected by military or governmental or economic power or church politics, no striving for mastery or domination over other people who simply disagree

---

1. Augustine, *City of God*, trans. Marcus Dods (New York: Random House, 1950), 352, book 11, section 9.

with us or have their own histories or opinions. None of that will survive the great transition between this world and that one. So why would we preserve any of that here? Why would we not live in anticipation of the day when we shall all be one in Jesus Christ?

And this, of course, is the second part of the vision. It is ultimately about God, and our relationship to God. As a Christian educator, I want the men and women who come my way to learn a great many things—ancient history, textual analysis, archaeology, biblical theology, and literature, and, if possible, some Hebrew and other Semitic languages. Those are basic requirements of my particular discipline. And you can insert your own materials into this list and make the same point.

But what I want even more is for them to catch in my work some glimpse of the much larger work of God. They will not see this merely in my preaching or in any cluster of pretty words I might manage to line up. They might see it in my life, and I hope for that. And they should see it in my work, or yours. They may hear the work of God in the magnificence of the counterpoint of Johann Sebastian Bach or see it in the elegance of a computer program that solves a major problem or in the success of a business plan that gives meaningful work to people who have not had it before. It's not just a question of baptizing what we were going to do anyway and pretending that it is somehow holy. It can be holy in fact when it connects to a deeper vision of who God is.

So now, today, let us seek this vision of a holy God who transforms us from a life choked and strangled by our own narrow ambitions into a more generous, more thoughtful, more active way of being that fits God's original vision for us. Let us leave behind the dark places of fear and run toward the heavenly mountain, the Jerusalem above, in which those who have gone before and those who will come after us may unite together before the throne of the One who still changes the world and promises to change each of us.

## A Prayer

O God, clothe us, not with shining golden robes that kings wear
nor stockbrokers' bespoke suits nor the little black dresses worn on
runways in Paris. Clothe us with hand-me-downs from righteous
people, the sort of clothes one would wear to the heavenly banquet. If we sneak into your party, receive us not as crashers but as
friends. For that is what we want to be. Amen.

# Afterword

And so we reach the end, for now. Jagged, disjointed, slightly argumentative and cranky as I now see, these meditations stand in a long tradition of piling up words that do not run away and hide when their fragmentary nature lies exposed, since life is about finding the true story among the seemingly meaningless sequence of one damned or blessed or merely inevitable thing after another. So we should not cower before the voices that cry for order, order, order. Order is overrated. Or rather, its preciousness comes from its rarity. Often disorder serves best to point to what has so far eluded us.

As Robert Penn Warren says, poetry is a way of life. And so is theology, and so is faith. What's more, there is a poetry of faith as it seeks not just to feel, but also to understand. Faith and understanding are far from being mortal enemies, as the Enlightenment mistakenly tried to teach us. Quite to the contrary, faith seeks to understand both its object and its subject. The believing person wishes to engage with God with all her being and to understand herself better as one who believes. All of the inquiry fits together. Or at least it can under the right circumstances.

In these short meditations, then, I have sought to help myself and anyone who reads them find a more comprehensive view of reality that rests on radical trust in God's goodness and mercy. Such a stance toward life allows one to search without fear, to question without regret, to doubt and then to believe. May we all do so.

www.ingramcontent.com/pod-product-compliance
Lightning Source LLC
Chambersburg PA
CBHW032232080426
42735CB00008B/827